CAMPAIGN 316

SHREWSBURY 1403

Struggle for a Fragile Crown

DICKON WHITEWOOD   ILLUSTRATED BY GRAHAM TURNER

Series editor Marcus Cowper

OSPREY PUBLISHING
Bloomsbury Publishing Plc

Kemp House, Chawley Park, Cumnor Hill, Oxford OX2 9PH, UK
29 Earlsfort Terrace, Dublin 2, Ireland
1385 Broadway, 5th Floor, New York, NY 10018, USA
Email: info@ospreypublishing.com
www.ospreypublishing.com

OSPREY is a trademark of Osprey Publishing Ltd

First published in Great Britain in 2017
Transferred to digital print in 2022

A catalogue record for this book is available from the British Library.

Print ISBN: 978 1 4728 2680 0
ePub: 978 1 4728 2679 4
ePDF: 978 1 4728 2678 7
XML: 978 1 4728 2681 7

Editorial by Ilios Publishing Ltd – www.iliospublishing.com
Typeset in Myriad Pro and Sabon
Maps by www.bounford.com
3D BEVs by The Black Spot
Page layouts by PDQ Digital Media Solutions, Bungay, UK
Printed and bound in India by Replika Press Private Ltd.

24 25 26 27 28   10 9 8 7 6 5

The Woodland Trust
Osprey Publishing supports the Woodland Trust, the UK's leading
woodland conservation charity.

www.ospreypublishing.com
To find out more about our authors and books visit our website. Here
you will find extracts, author interviews, details of forthcoming events
and the option to sign-up for our newsletter.

AUTHOR'S DEDICATION

To my parents for all their love, help and encouragement.

ACKNOWLEDGEMENT

The author would like to express his sincere thanks to the following for
their assistance and courtesy: Keith Dowen of the Royal Armouries, Philip
Morgan of Keele University, Tobias Capwell of the Wallace Collection,
Matthew Strickland of Glasgow University, colleagues and friends at
Norfolk Museums Service, staff in the British Library, Marcus Cowper of Ilios
Publishing, and Bruce Hardy for kindly agreeing to look over the text.

ARTIST'S NOTE

Readers may care to note that the original paintings from which the colour
plates in this book were prepared are available for private sale.
The Publishers retain all reproduction copyright whatsoever.
All enquiries should be addressed to:

Graham Turner, PO Box 568, Aylesbury, Bucks, HP17 8EX, UK
www.studio88.co.uk

The Publishers regret that they can enter into no correspondence upon
this matter.

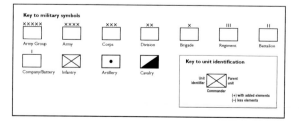

CONTENTS

England, 1403

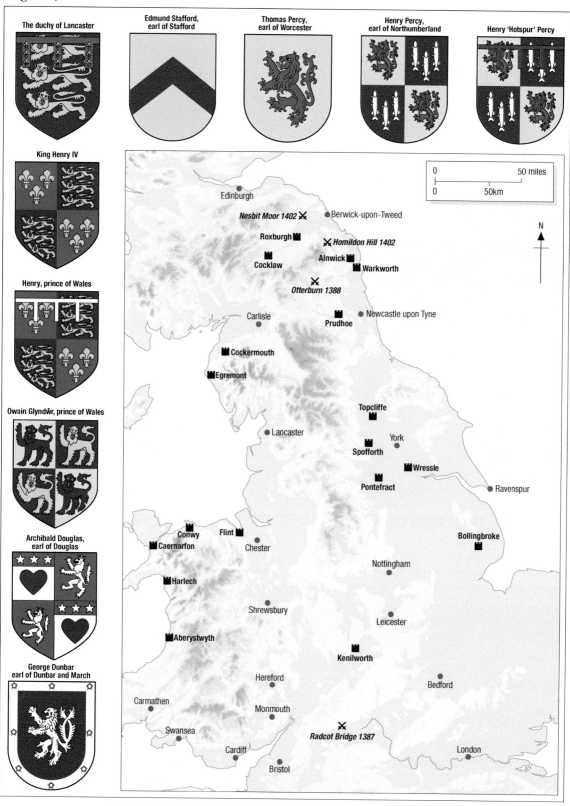

The duchy of Lancaster

Edmund Stafford, earl of Stafford

Thomas Percy, earl of Worcester

Henry Percy, earl of Northumberland

Henry 'Hotspur' Percy

King Henry IV

Henry, prince of Wales

Owain Glyndŵr, prince of Wales

Archibald Douglas, earl of Douglas

George Dunbar earl of Dunbar and March

0   50 miles
0   50km

N

Edinburgh

Nesbit Moor 1402   Berwick-upon-Tweed

Roxburgh   Homildon Hill 1402

Cocklaw   Alnwick   Warkworth

Otterburn 1388

Carlisle   Prudhoe   Newcastle upon Tyne

Cockermouth

Egremont

Topcliffe

Lancaster

York
Spofforth

Wressle

Pontefract   Ravenspur

Conwy   Flint
Caernarfon   Chester   Bollingbroke

Harlech

Nottingham

Shrewsbury

Leicester

Aberystwyth

Kenilworth

Hereford   Bedford

Carmathen

Monmouth

Swansea   Radcot Bridge 1387

Cardiff   London

Bristol

ORIGINS OF THE CAMPAIGN

In 1399, Henry of Bolingbroke deposed his cousin Richard II and was crowned king of England. His coronation was the culmination of a remarkable series of events and a drastic reversal of fortune. A year earlier, in September 1398, Henry had been exiled for ten years by the king in revenge for his role in the Lords Appellant rising of 1387–88, instigated by a group of the leading nobility to remove the king's court favourites and restrain his increasingly tyrannical rule. Although the rising had succeeded, the Appellants had made themselves implacable enemies of the king. By 1397, Richard had re-established his authority and felt secure enough to revenge himself upon the Appellants, who were systematically arrested and destroyed. In February 1399, while Henry was serving his exile in France, his father John of Gaunt, duke of Lancaster, died. Richard pounced upon the sudden opportunity and increased Henry's sentence to life, taking the vast duchy lands into his control. In order to regain his inheritance, Henry returned to England in July while Richard was away on campaign in Ireland. Landing at Ravenspur in Yorkshire with a handful of retainers, Henry was soon joined by a number of Lancastrian knights and other magnates determined to support his claim. Among the first was Henry Percy, earl of Northumberland, and his son Hotspur, two of the most powerful men in northern England, who after meeting with Bolingbroke at Bridlington, became active and influential participants in the following campaign.

Richard II came to the throne in 1377 following the deaths of his father, the Black Prince, and grandfather, Edward III. Although Richard showed early promise, his reign ended in failure. (Author's collection)

The army that flocked to Henry's banner was soon several thousand strong. Its command was awarded to Northumberland, whose active support was crucial to providing early impetus to Henry's cause. Over the next few weeks, the army progressed south to Bristol, where several of Richard's closest supporters had taken refuge. During the march, it soon became clear that Richard's support in England was evaporating. An army that had been raised to oppose Bolingbroke by Edmund, duke of York, chose instead to support him and was incorporated into Henry's forces. When Henry reached Bristol, the king's adherents were surrendered by the garrison and all but one was executed. King Richard returned from Ireland in late July and made his way to Conwy Castle in north Wales, hoping to raise an army. It soon became clear that his hopes of resisting Bolingbroke

Henry Percy, earl of Northumberland takes Richard II prisoner. The Percys took an active part in Henry IV's usurpation of 1399 and were heavily rewarded by the new king following his coronation. (British Library, Ms. Harley 1319, f. 44)

were futile, and on 12 August he was persuaded to leave the safety of the castle by the assurances of the earl of Northumberland. Once Richard was outside the walls, however, he was quickly ambushed, taken into custody and forced to accompany the earl to Flint Castle, where the two men were joined by Bolingbroke himself. Richard was then transported to the Tower of London, but not before Hotspur had underlined the Percys' importance to the campaign by defeating a force of dissident Cheshiremen intent on releasing the king from captivity.

Richard was formally denounced in Parliament on 1 October 1399, leaving the path clear for Bolingbroke to claim the throne and be crowned, which happened on 13 October, the feast day of Edward the Confessor. Meanwhile, Richard was kept in custody at the Tower before being transported to Pontefract Castle where, on 14 February 1400, he died, reportedly by being starved to death.

Henry's success in gaining the throne had been dependent in no small measure on the support of the Percy family. In 1399, the Percy family consisted of three main players: Henry Percy, earl of Northumberland; his son, also named Henry but better known by his famous *nom de guerre* 'Hotspur'; and Northumberland's brother, Thomas, earl of Worcester. Together, these three men constituted the greatest family in northern England, with extensive properties in Northumberland, Yorkshire and Cumberland. Among their estates they could boast of castles at Alnwick, Warkworth, Wressle, Cockermouth, Egremont, Prudhoe, Topcliffe and Spofforth, as well as numerous other smaller manors. Many of these properties had been added to their portfolio during the previous century, with those in Cumberland gained most recently through the elder Henry's marriage to Maud, baroness Lucy, in 1381. In recognition of his standing, Henry Percy was created earl of Northumberland during Richard II's coronation celebrations on 16 July 1377, a title that elevated him above all his immediate northern rivals, including the Nevilles of Raby.

The Percys were highly jealous of their position in the north and closely guarded important offices of state such as the two wardenships on the Scottish border, positions that came with extensive powers and salaries. Percy ambitions in the region occasionally caused disagreements with the Crown and other members of the nobility. In 1381, Northumberland and John of Gaunt became engaged in a public quarrel that had its origins in the Percys' territorial concerns and the resentment they felt toward Gaunt's appointment as royal lieutenant in the area. In the late 1390s, the Percys' relationship with Richard II deteriorated when he began to pursue a policy aimed at securing a permanent peace with Scotland, precluding their long-established hope of territorial expansion within Scotland. Percy discontent was reinforced by Richard's simultaneous display of favour towards Ralph

Neville, 4th baron Neville de Raby. In 1396, the Percys lost control of the West March to Neville who, at the same time, was granted the important manors of Penrith and Sowerby in Cumberland, two estates that had long been coveted by Northumberland himself. Neville was further rewarded, to the Percys' consternation, by his promotion to the earldom of Westmorland on 29 September 1397, in a grand ceremony which also saw Thomas Percy was elevated to the earldom of Worcester. This development posed a distinct threat to the Percys' pre-eminence in the north and was guaranteed to provoke a reaction. Discord between the Percys and Richard II climaxed in 1399, in which year the chronicler Jean Froissart records that Northumberland and Hotspur were banished and forced to take refuge in Scotland. Although there is no substantive evidence to support these claims, the report amply demonstrates the frosty relations between the Percys and Richard II in existence prior to Bolingbroke's invasion.

It is likely that the Percys saw their support for Henry as an opportunity to further their political aims on the northern border and remove the significant threat posed to them by Richard II. It was fortunate for the Percys that the political landscape in 1399 was highly favourable to their taking on a more prominent position in national affairs. The leading nobility had been divided in their support for Richard II and many of those who opposed him, such as the Lords Appellant, had been destroyed. When Henry IV was crowned, the number of prominent nobles who could be relied upon by the Lancastrian regime was further reduced, since those such as John Montagu, earl of Salisbury, John Holland, duke of Exeter, Thomas Holland, duke of Surrey and Thomas Despenser, earl of Gloucester, had been close supporters of the former king. In 1400, these four men became engaged in a plot, known as the Epiphany Rising, to seize and kill Henry IV during a tournament at Windsor and reinstate the captive Richard on the throne. The plan was betrayed to the king by Edmund, earl of Rutland, and although the flag of rebellion was raised, the effort failed to attract any significant support. Many of the ringleaders were soon apprehended and executed by lynch mobs, or beheaded following quickly arranged and makeshift trials.

Henry IV's coronation at Westminster Abbey on 13 October 1399. (British Library, Ms. Harley 4380, f. 168v)

The effect of these events was the drastic reduction in the number of adult nobility able to take part in the governance of the realm. The Percys, unscathed from these upheavals, were ideally placed to exploit the resulting vacuum.

On 30 September 1399, Northumberland was named constable of England for life. Soon after, both Hotspur and Northumberland were granted office as wardens of the east and west March on the border with Scotland. These posts came with substantial stipends. In times of peace or truce the earl received £1,500 a year, rising to £6,000 in times of war. Hotspur, in control of the more strategically important East March, received a larger salary of £3,000 and £12,000 respectively. Percy power in the north was further expanded

A picture of Alnwick Castle in Northumberland from across the river Aln. The Percy family purchased Alnwick in 1309, transforming it into one of the strongest castles on the Anglo-Scottish border. It has remained the seat of the Percy earls of Northumberland to the present day. (Author's photograph)

when Hotspur was granted the captaincy of Roxburgh Castle and the custody of Bamburgh Castle for life, on 24 October 1399.

At the same time, the Percys made extensive gains outside of their traditional northern sphere of influence. On 19 October, Northumberland was granted the Isle of Man for himself and his heirs, and on the 24th Hotspur was given office, power and land in North Wales. He was made justice of Cheshire, North Wales and Flintshire, constable of the castles of Chester, Flint, Conwy and Caernarfon, and received the county and lordship of Anglesey for life, along with the castle of Beaumaris. The Percys' interest in Wales was further expanded on 17 November when Northumberland received a portion of the Mortimer estates during the minority of Edmund Mortimer, earl of March.

Thomas Percy was also rewarded by Henry. The grants he had received from Edward III and Richard II were confirmed, he was given 500 marks a year for life and, in November 1399, he gained the position of admiral of

The keep of Warkworth Castle was begun by the 1st earl of Northumberland as part of a wide range of improvement works. The castle's surviving fabric remains much the same as it was when first built. (Author's photograph)

England. In March 1401, he was reinstated in his position under Richard II as steward of the household and became an active member of the king's council, crucial to the government of the realm and frequently employed on diplomatic missions. As soon as 12 October 1399 he was entrusted by Henry IV, who described him warmly as 'our very dear and faithful cousin', to renew the truce between England and France and to negotiate a royal marriage.

The scale of the rewards the Percys received was vast, extending their control on the northern border to an unprecedented level and providing them with power and wealth in areas where they had hitherto shown little interest. Percy gains were also far greater in scale and importance than those awarded to any of Henry IV's other supporters who had joined him in 1399, including the earl of Westmorland. The reason appears to have been the extraordinary nature of their contribution to Henry's crown-winning campaign and the gratitude the king naturally felt towards them. The Percys, for their part, may have felt that the grants were a rightful recognition of their role as principal kingmakers.

The most remarkable aspect of the Percy ascendancy, however, proved to be its transitory nature. By 1403, less than four years after Henry IV's coronation, their relationship with the king had deteriorated to such an extent that they decided to reverse their policy of 1399 and lead a rebellion against the Lancastrian regime, culminating in the battle of Shrewsbury. Two further rebellions would be launched in 1405 and 1408 that together brought utter, albeit temporary, ruin to the family. Historians have long speculated on the reasons behind the Percys' estrangement towards Henry IV and the Lancastrian government. The difficulty has lain in the fact that there does not appear to have been a single, decisive factor to blame for such a serious breakdown in relations. Instead, Percy discontent was a result of the cumulative effect of many competing grievances and deteriorating personal relationships that, by 1403, had created an irreparable breach between the Percys and the king.

One cause of strain was financial, and both Northumberland and Hotspur appear to have become increasingly frustrated by the king's failure to pay the money they felt due to them, either in full or as promptly as each required. The *Eulogium Historiarum* preserves an account of a confrontation between Northumberland and the king, in which Percy demanded money for the defence of the marches, and the king angrily replied, 'I have no money and you will receive none!' More direct proof of Percy grievances come from the written requests they sent to the king. In May 1401, Hotspur wrote to Henry's council twice to complain that his soldiers in Wales and North England were without their pay. On 4 June, the problem in Wales had seemingly worsened for he wrote again, this time in more desperate terms, suggesting that he would have to quit the country entirely if £5,000 was not allocated to him immediately, 'which becomes a matter of necessity to me for I cannot bear the costs I am at'. In order to ensure his soldiers were paid, Hotspur was often forced to finance their costs out of his own pocket. On some occasions, there also appear to have been problems extracting additional revenues to which he was entitled and, on 3 July 1401, he complained in strong terms regarding the difficulties he faced in extracting revenues from the customs of London, Hull and Boston.

The earl of Northumberland was equally vociferous in his financial complaints. On 30 May 1403, he repeated his son's protest that his soldiers were without their pay. Another letter, sent on 26 June and only a few weeks before the rebellion, denied a claim that £60,000 had been granted to them since the king's coronation and insisted that he and his son were still owed £20,000 for services rendered in the north and in Wales. This figure is likely

The Percy lion on the keep of Alnwick Castle. Although the Percy family had been involved in northern politics and border warfare for several hundred years, their domination on the East March was a product of their success and territorial acquisitions during the 14th century. (Author's photograph)

The ruins of Roxburgh Castle sit atop a high mound overlooking the congruence of the rivers Tweed and Teviot. Hotspur was granted the constableship of the castle in 1399, giving the Percys complete control of border affairs. (Author's collection)

to have been an exaggeration. It has been estimated by J. M. W Bean that in the period 1399–1403, a total of £38,591 was provided to the Percys by the Crown, indicating rather more extensive financial support towards them than their letters suggest.

Conversely, however, it has been argued by Cynthia Neville that Henry IV deliberately withheld payment to the Percys while ensuring swift recompense to Ralph Neville. Whatever the truth of this, it is clear that the Percys felt themselves to be economically disadvantaged by Henry and resented the frequent need to finance their military service to him themselves, even if this only caused them a temporary inconvenience. The Percys' financial grievances were, however, no doubt worsened by another fiscal policy adopted by Henry IV aimed at securing his throne. In order to build the Lancastrian retinue following his coronation, Henry began to distribute annuities among the landed gentry, which amounted to £24,000 annually and a total of £120,000 over the period 1399–1403. Such payments must have irritated the Percys as their own need for money, spent in the defence of Henry's kingdom, was arguably far more pressing.

Some of the king's financial difficulties were outside of his control, caused by war, the outbreak of which Henry had no part. In September 1400, a rebellion began in Wales that had its origins in a minor dispute between Owain Glyndŵr, the native lord of Glyndyfrdwy and Cynllaith, and his regional English rival Reginald, Lord Grey of Ruthin. On 18 September a Welsh attack was made on Ruthin and other English towns in North Wales. Although the Welsh suffered a defeat on the 24th, this minor setback had little effect on the spread of the revolt. A punitive campaign launched by Henry IV in October also had little impact, as the Welsh resorted to the tried and tested tactics of avoiding contact with the English army as it progressed through the Welsh lowlands. These events soon involved the Percys, due to the grants awarded to Hotspur in Wales. At Easter 1401 Conwy Castle, one of the fortifications under Hotspur's command, was captured by Rhys and Gwilym ap Tudur. After conducting the siege to retake it, at which Prince

Henry, later Henry V, was present, Hotspur remained in north Wales for the rest of the summer, co-ordinating the English attacks against Glyndŵr's forces.

In March 1402, Henry IV responded to the ever-worsening and costly Welsh rising by making Hotspur and Thomas Percy royal lieutenants in north and south Wales. Later that year, however, an English force was heavily defeated at the battle of Pilleth (Bryn Glas) and their commander Edmund Mortimer, uncle to the earl of March, taken as Glyndŵr's captive. The Percys were related to the Mortimer family through Hotpur's marriage to Elizabeth, Edmund's sister. Hotspur therefore requested permission from the king to pay his brother-in-law's ransom. This created a source of tension as Edmund's capture was politically convenient to the Lancastrian regime. Henry's coronation had been contentious, not only because of the usurpation of Richard II, but also because the rival claims of the young Mortimer earl of March (also named Edmund) had been ignored in order to place Henry on the throne. Many contemporaries felt that this political manipulation was unjust, and some chronicles suggest that Hotspur himself was among those angered at the proceedings, excusing himself from Henry's coronation feast in protest. While March was in his minority, the older Edmund was the effective head of the Mortimer family. His capture, therefore, temporarily removed a potential threat to Henry that the king was happy to keep dormant. Hotspur's request was denied.

Later in 1402, both Hotspur and Worcester lost their Welsh commands and were replaced by Prince Henry and a circle of his advisors. Other important positions lost the same year included Hotspur's captaincy of Roxburgh Castle, awarded to Ralph Neville, and Worcester's role as steward of the royal household. In addition to these sackings, other grievances were beginning to fester. The available evidence suggests that the Percys were in fundamental disagreement with the king over his stance towards the Welsh rebellion. They had come to believe that a military solution to the revolt was going to be difficult, if not impossible, to achieve and so advocated a rapprochement with Glyndŵr. While in Wales, Hotspur had gone so far as to meet with the Welsh leader in order to discuss terms, which Glyndŵr was reportedly willing to consider. The king, however, was uncompromising, even going as far as to angrily berate Hotspur for his failure to apprehend Glyndŵr when he had the opportunity.

It is likely that one of reasons behind the Percys' attitude towards Wales was their wish to focus their attentions on the north which,

The seal of Henry Percy, earl of Northumberland after his marriage to Maude Lucy in 1381. Northumberland spent his career increasing the political and territorial power of the Percy family, and fiercely defended his family's interests on several occasions in the late 14th century. (Society of Antiquaries)

Ralph Neville was the Percy's main rival in northern England. In 1396 he married Henry Bolingbroke's half-sister, Joan Beaufort, and was rewarded by Henry after his coronation. His tomb and monumental effigy lies in St Mary's Church in Staindrop, Co Durham. (Author's collection)

in 1402, was a centre of political and military activity. In addition to the king showing favour to Ralph Neville, another potential rival to the Percys was George Dunbar, the Scottish earl of March, who had defected to Henry IV early in his reign and who had competing claims for the king's favour in the area. Dunbar was one of the foremost soldiers of his day and, on 22 June 1402, he defeated an incursion into England by his fellow countrymen at the battle of Nisbet Moor. Another, more serious concern, was the increased threat from Scotland itself. The Percys' main rival across the border, as well as Dunbar's, was Archibald, earl of Douglas. In August 1402, Douglas led a full-scale raid into England but on his return to Scotland, laden with booty, he was waylaid by an English army commanded by the earl of Northumberland and Hotspur, with Dunbar in the role of advisor. The battle of Homildon Hill was fought on 14 September and resulted in an overwhelming victory for the Percys. Five earls, including Douglas, were captured along with at least 30 other Scottish knights, most of whom came from the Scottish borders.

In usual circumstances, the victors of a battle could expect to dictate the terms of their captive's release. However, on 20 September, the king wrote to the Percys prohibiting the ransom or return of any of the prisoners, except on his authority. Instead, he ordered that they should be brought to Westminster where a Parliament was to be convened a week later. These terms were bitterly resented by the Percys and, while Northumberland complied, Hotspur refused outright to part with his captives, the most important of whom was Douglas himself. Hotspur may have felt that the ransom from his captives was his to dictate, and too great a prize to hand over to the king's arbitration. Additionally, we cannot exclude the possibility that he had other, more personal, concerns. The Percys had a long-standing rivalry with the Douglases and Archibald's capture, therefore, represented a personal triumph for Hotspur, which also did much to revenge his own capture by the Scots following the battle of Otterburn in 1388.

Hotspur's recalcitrant attitude can also be interpreted as a direct response to Henry's own continued refusal to allow the ransom of Edmund Mortimer. The king's attitude to Mortimer was especially controversial, as he himself had acted swiftly to ensure payment for Lord Grey's ransom when he was taken prisoner by Glyndŵr in January 1402. Fuelled by rumours of treachery and even in the complicity of Mortimer in his own capture, the king had come to believe that he was a traitor to the Crown, and had consequently ordered Mortimer's property to be confiscated. Perhaps reacting to this news, in November 1402 Mortimer married Catrin, Glyndŵr's daughter, and two weeks later wrote to his vassals declaring that he would henceforth fight for his father-in-law's rights in Wales. To the king, these actions justified the suspicions he had held, but to Hotspur it must have appeared that the king had forced Mortimer into his actions by refusing Hotspur permission to pay his ransom.

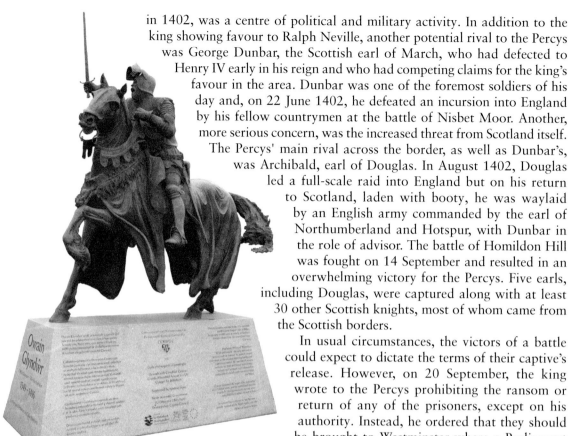

Beginning as a local quarrel, Owain Glyndŵr's uprising became increasingly problematic for the English administration in Wales. In 1403 the revolt became national. This statue of Glyndŵr in Corwen, Denbighshire captures some of the heroism often attributed to the semi-mythical figure. (Author's photograph)

In October 1402 Parliament was convened to discuss the Scottish captives taken at Homildon Hill. Northumberland presented his prisoners as requested, but the absence of Douglas must have been obvious and the king was understandably angered. Northumberland, for his part, questioned Henry about his inability to pay the Percys for their military services. Hotspur seems to have visited the king in person soon after, perhaps urged to do so by his father. Two conflicting accounts of the meeting survive. According to the *Brut* chronicle Hotspur came to the king to enquire about the money that was still behind for the keeping of the marches, but received an evasive reply in return. Angered at this, Hotspur accused the king of lying in 1399 as to his real intentions towards taking the Crown. Henry became incensed at this provocation and moved forward, striking Hotspur on the face. Equally enraged, Hotspur angrily shouted, 'wel this shal be the shrewdest bofet that ever thow yovyst'. In the *English Chronicle* the account differs, by suggesting Mortimer's ransom was the cause of the disagreement. Hotspur began by asking the king, 'Shall a man spend his goods and put himself in peril for you and your realm and you will not help him in his need?' Now that the king regarded Mortimer as a traitor, however, this argument was unlikely to sway him. Tempers rising, Henry accused Hotspur of treachery on the basis that Hotspur was asking favour for Henry's enemies and those of the realm. The king then drew his dagger, provoking Hotspur to issue the challenge, 'Not here but in the field!'

The chroniclers suggest that once Hotspur removed himself from the king's presence he immediately began to ferment and plan rebellion. In reality, however, hostilities were still several months away. Further doubt is placed on the veracity of these accounts by a subsequent grant awarded to the Percys by the king that, far from showing a breakdown, tends instead to suggest the continued importance Henry attached to keeping them content and within royal favour. On 2 March 1403, for his victory at Homildon Hill

The site of the battle of Homildon (or Humbleton) Hill near Wooler in Northumberland. The Scots deployed in a strong defensive schiltron formation above the line of trees in the centre of the picture. The English began the battle on the flat ground below. (Author's photograph)

and other 'great labours' in Scotland, Northumberland was gifted the earldom of Douglas in its entirety, including Eskdale, Liddesdale, Lauderdale, Selkirk, Ettick Forest and Teviotdale. The grant of these lands, however, while in theory exponentially increasing Percy power in the north, was not in Henry's power to award. It is also highly unlikely that the king had consulted with other regional powers, such as Westmorland and Dunbar, not to mention the captive earl of Douglas or Robert III, king of Scotland, within whose kingdom the earldom was situated.

The Percys' attitude to the grant, which could only be achieved through their personal military endeavour, is unclear. Whatever their thoughts on the feasibility of the grant, the Percys reacted in the spring of 1403 by launching a campaign into Scotland, centred around the castle of Cocklaw, near the town of Hawick. The Scottish garrison refused to surrender, but agreed that if they had not been relieved by forces under the Scots regent, Robert, duke of Albany, they would surrender the castle by 1 August. Albany was reported to be assembling an army to respond to English aggression, and it has been suggested that the prospect of having to face a full-scale Scottish royal army was a greater challenge than the Percys had anticipated. However, given their total success at Homildon Hill, it seems unlikely that they would have baulked at the prospect of another battle which, if victorious, would leave their conquest of the earldom of Douglas open. Instead, financial difficulties appear to have held the Percys back from further military effort, and on 26

A romanticized picture of the battle of Homildon Hill from Cassell's *History of England*. In reality, the Percy men-at-arms and cavalry had little to do, thanks to the deadly efficiency of the English longbowmen. (Author's collection)

The physical confrontation between Henry IV and Hotspur is pictured here in a 15th-century manuscript. On the left is the resulting Battle of Shrewsbury. (Walters Art Museum, Ms. W201, f. 283)

According to the Scottish chronicler Walter Bower, Hotspur wanted to lead an immediate cavalry charge against the Scots at Homildon Hill, but was reluctantly persuaded against the manoeuvre by George Dunbar. This statue of Hotspur at Alnwick Castle, depicted on horseback with lance in hand, captures the spirit of his impetuous character. (Author's photograph)

June the earl of Northumberland sent a letter to the king from Healaugh in Yorkshire, demanding that funds be sent immediately if dishonour to the realm, and the Percys themselves, was to be avoided. Couched in grand language this effectively meant that the Percys could not support their Scottish ambitions without receiving more money from the exchequer. King Henry, however, appears never to have intended or promised to finance the Percy campaign. Furthermore, and contrary to Percy claims, the king made it clear that he considered the funds the Crown had already supplied to be more than adequate for the defence of the border in its current position.

It must have become obvious to the Percys that without the cash to support their campaign, the Douglas grant was worth little more than the parchment it was written on. If this realization was the immediate cause of the revolt that began in July 1403, or whether the Percys had been planning the rebellion over a longer time, as their dissatisfaction with Henry IV grew, will never be known. What is beyond doubt, however, is that in early July Hotspur arrived suddenly in Chester and proclaimed a general rising against Henry IV and the Lancastrian government. The revolt had begun.

CHRONOLOGY

1377	Accession of Richard II.
1387–88	The Lords Appellant defeat Robert de Vere at the battle of Radcot Bridge. In the following 'Merciless Parliament' many members of Richard II's household are put to death and his authority restrained.
1388	Battle of Otterburn. Hotspur is defeated and captured by the Scots.
1398	Bolingbroke is exiled by Richard II.
1399	Bolingbroke returns, deposes Richard II and is crowned king. The Percys are heavily rewarded for their part in the rebellion.
1400	The revolt of Owain Glyndŵr breaks out in Wales.
1402	
21 June	Battle of Bryn Glas. The Welsh defeat and capture Edmund Mortimer, Hotspur's brother-in-law.
22 June	Battle of Nesbit Moor. George Dunbar defeats a Scottish raid.
14 September	Battle of Homildon Hill. The Percys defeat the Scots under Archibald Douglas, 4th earl of Douglas. Prisoners include five earls, including Douglas, and a great array of Scottish knights.
20 September	Henry IV writes to the Percys, refusing them permission to ransom the Scottish prisoners without his permission. Hotspur retains the custody of Douglas against the king's orders.
1403	
2 March	Henry IV grants the earl of Northumberland the earldom of Douglas and great swathes of land in Scotland.
April	Hotspur moves into Scotland and besieges Cocklaw Tower, near Hawick.
May	Prince Henry launches a campaign in Wales and burns Glyndŵr's manors of Sycarth and Glyndyfrdwy.
3–12 July	Owain Glyndŵr marches down the Tywi Valley taking English-held towns and castles. A force of 700 Welshmen is destroyed by Lord Carew.
9 July	Hotspur arrives in Chester and raises the flag of rebellion.
12–14 July	Henry IV, moving north to aid the Percys against the Scots, hears news of the rebellion.

17 July	Hotspur assembles his army at Sandiway.
20 July	Worcester defects from the prince and joins with Hotspur, taking part of the Shrewsbury garrison with him.
21 July	Battle of Shrewsbury. Hotspur and the rebel army are defeated by Henry IV.
22–23 July	Hotspur's body is taken by Thomas Neville, Lord Furnival and buried in Whitchurch. It is exhumed on Henry IV's orders and publicly displayed.
23 July	Execution of Thomas Percy, earl of Worcester, and other rebels.
11 August	Northumberland is taken prisoner by Henry IV in York.
1404	
January	Warkworth, Alnwick and Berwick refuse to surrender to Henry IV. Northumberland receives a full pardon and is restored to his estates.
Summer	The Welsh high tide. Glyndŵr captures Harlech and Aberystwyth and holds his first parliament in Machynlleth, where he is crowned prince of Wales.
1405	
February	Signing of the Tripartite Indenture between Northumberland, Glyndŵr and Edmund Mortimer agreeing, in principle, to divide the kingdom between them.
27 May–8 June	The rebellion of Richard Scrope, archbishop of York, fails. The archbishop, Thomas de Mowbray, 4th earl of Norfolk, and other rebels are executed.
1408	
19 February	Northumberland returns to England and is killed at the battle of Bramham Moor.
1412	The end of Glyndŵr's rebellion.

OPPOSING COMMANDERS

THE REBEL ARMY

Henry Percy, son of Henry, earl of Northumberland and Margaret Neville, was born on 20 May 1364. A second cousin of Henry IV, Hotspur first experienced warfare aged nine when he accompanied his father on campaign in France. In 1378, at the age of 12, he engaged in his first military combat when a group of Scots surprised and took the town of Berwick. The earl of Northumberland raced north and, after a siege of nine days, allowed his son to lead the assault, during which the town was duly retaken. Militarily the young Henry had come of age. According to the English chronicler Thomas Walsingham, Henry was 'constantly active' from this day, 'especially against the Scots, whom he subdued with tireless courage at every outbreak of disorder. On account of this, they called him Haatspore.' Nor were the Scots the only ones to feel the force of Hotspur's restless energy. In 1383, Froissart records that he travelled to Prussia, hoping to fight alongside the Teutonic Knights on their crusade in Lithuania. In 1385, he joined Richard II's invasion of Scotland and in 1386 he was in Calais, where he succeeded in 'making his name as feared by the French on the seas as by the Scots on the Border.' He used the town as a base to conduct a series of raids, carrying off booty and performing such feats of arms that the 'King of France decided against taking direct possession of the town of Calais, but thought it better to treat with England'. Hotspur was fast becoming a chivalric idol and an example to others. This later caused Shakespeare to eulogise him, that 'by his light did all the chivalry of England move to do brave acts'.

Early in 1388, he was made a knight of the Garter and warden of the East March. Later that year, the Scots launched a massive raid into England under the leadership of James, earl of Douglas. Hotspur moved to intercept them and at Otterburn, in Redesdale, the armies clashed as the night descended. Fighting in the dark, the confused battle that resulted ended in the capture of Hotspur and the death of Douglas – and became known as 'the battle a dead man won'. Hotspur was soon ransomed at the price of 3000*l*, a third of which was paid by parliament. Hotspur joined Henry of Bolingbroke's retinue at the jousts of St Inglevert

Hotspur's personal bravery and military exploits had made him a popular chivalric figure during his own lifetime. He would later gain everlasting fame through his part in Shakespeare's *Henry IV, Part I*. (Author's photograph)

SIMPLIFIED GENEALOGICAL TREE
Showing the lineage and relationships between those involved in the
Battle of Shrewsbury

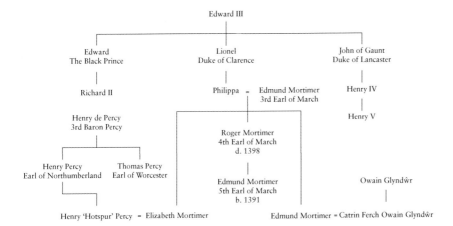

and participated in the tournament at Smithfield in 1390. In 1393, Hotspur
was sent on a diplomatic mission to James, king of Cyprus, and later served
as lieutenant of Aquitaine as the deputy of John of Gaunt.

Hotspur's military activity in service of Henry IV increased his body of
experience and added to his reputation as a military man. His abilities as
a commander, however, as opposed to his undoubted individual skills, are
more open to debate. At Homildon Hill in 1402, the Scots had decided to
take up a position at the top of a readily defensible incline, strengthening
their already formidable situation by forming into a protective schiltron
formation, their pikes bristling and facing out ready for an English attack.
According to Walter Bower's *Scottichronicon*, Hotspur was itching for an
all-out cavalry charge up the hill but was reluctantly persuaded against this
rash action by George Dunbar. Irrespective of the truth of this account, it
highlights the impetuous aspect of Hotspur's character, often remarked upon
by contemporaries. While this attribute had made Hotspur a chivalric hero,
it also had the potential to limit his ability as a battlefield commander.

Hotspur's uncle, **Thomas Percy, earl of Worcester,** was an experienced
soldier, diplomat and household officer with a history of service going back to
the reign of Edward III. Born *c*.1343, he saw active military service in France
and Spain during the Hundred Years War and may have fought for the Black
Prince at Nájera in 1367. From 1369 he is frequently mentioned in Froissart's
Chronicles, fighting alongside other famous knights such as Sir John
Chandos and Sir Robert Knolles. In 1370 and 1371 he served on a
number of campaigns, including the siege and sack of Limoges in
September 1370, again under the Black Prince. In 1372 he was
captured in a naval engagement near Soubise, receiving his final
release in 1374. Thomas was actively employed by
both Richard II and Henry IV and was suitably
rewarded by both monarchs.
He was under-chamberlain of
Richard's household from 1390
to 1393 and steward from 1393

A rowel spur dating to the
early 15th century, used by
riders to encourage their
mount onwards. The sobriquet
'Hotspur' was used during
Henry Percy's lifetime, given
to him by the Scots for his
tenacity on the border. (Royal
Armouries, VI.386)

to 1399, often attending the king's council and witnessing royal charters. He accompanied Richard to Ireland in 1395 and 1399, served on missions to France and was justiciar of south Wales in 1390–99. After defecting to Henry IV in 1399, his career continued to flourish. There is little reason to believe that this history of service and reward was about to cease in 1403 and his involvement in the rebellion therefore shocked and confused contemporaries. Walsingham says that 'no whisper of treachery had ever before been breathed [by Worcester] in all his life, the man who alone among Englishmen earned such a renown for honesty, that the kings of France and Spain trusted his mere word, in treaties and agreements, more than the written signature of anyone.' The monk of Saint-Denys believed he was 'tormented by his notorious betrayal of Richard II' and motivated by 'tardy remorse'. It is more probable, however, that family loyalty as much as any other consideration compelled him to join Hotspur in 1403. Worcester's involvement in the initial planning of the campaign is uncertain, but once he had committed to the rebel cause, his presence provided the army with a proven soldier and field commander, adding considerably to its military threat.

One of the more surprising participants in the battle, fighting on the rebel side, was **Archibald, earl of Douglas**. In previous years, he had been a resolute rival to the Percys, and as recently as a few weeks before the start of the campaign had been their prisoner. The reason for Douglas' involvement probably lies in a deal done between himself and Hotspur, perhaps involving the waiver of his ransom and a promise by the Percys to respect his lands in Scotland. Douglas must also have been tempted by the possibility of fighting his territorial rival, George Dunbar. Aged 34 at Shrewsbury, Douglas was a physically impressive warrior, despite the loss of an eye at Homildon Hill. Although his most recent battle had ended in defeat, he had himself won a

Archibald Douglas's father had inherited the earldom of Douglas following the death of James, earl of Douglas, at the battle of Otterburn in 1388. Although James was killed, Hotspur was taken prisoner. This stone commemorates the site of the battle in Redesdale, Northumberland. Archibald inherited the earldom from his father in 1400. (Author's photograph)

small victory over Hotspur and Dunbar in 1401. His unfortunate military record later gained him the title of 'Tyneman' (loser), but many of these defeats were largely outside of his control.

Two men who were not present at the battle but had an impact on the campaign were **Henry Percy, earl of Northumberland,** and **Owain Glyndŵr.** Northumberland was the head of the Percy family and had spent his life strengthening their position in the north, acquiring new estates and propelling the family into the first ranks of the English nobility. He directed Percy policy and it was his intervention in 1399 that had proved critical to Henry IV's success and the Percys' political ascension. There can be little doubt that he was involved in the rebellion from the start. Glyndŵr's role in the Percy rebellion is less clear, but considering that both he and the Percys shared Henry IV as a common enemy, the benefits of cooperation were obvious. Glyndŵr was descended from impeccable Welsh princely stock. The poet Iolo Goch in a celebrated *cywydd* (metrical poem) traced his pedigree in the paternal line to Bleddyn ap Cynfyn, prince of Powys (d. 1075), and in the maternal line to Rhys ap Tewdwr, prince of Deheubarth (d. 1093). His upbringing was typical for a man of his rank, serving in English military expeditions in Scotland and France. Glyndŵr's revolt represented a break with his family's past service to the Crown and began with a local dispute between him and his neighbour Lord Grey. Even after several years of rebellion, it appears that Glyndŵr had not become a diehard rebel and was open to the possibility of returning to his traditional loyalty. However, as a result of Henry IV's attitude, Glyndŵr was forced to continue the rebellion and secure his future the only way left to him: making the revolt truly national and removing all vestiges of English power within Wales.

THE ROYAL ARMY

In his *Constitutional History of England*, the historian and bishop William Stubbs declared of **Henry IV**, 'there is scarcely one in the whole line of our kings of whose personality it is so difficult to get a general idea'. Stubbs nevertheless recognized him as a 'great man' whose repeated triumphs over adversity provided a strong platform for the later glories of the Lancastrian dynasty.

Henry's career was not one on which tales of glory could easily be based. From 1377, Henry was heavily enmeshed in the intrigues prevalent during the tumultuous reign of Richard II. In 1399 he gained his throne by deposing his cousin, and was then implicit in Richard's murder at Pontefract Castle. Henry's subsequent reign was beset by rebellions, illness and disagreements with his closest relations. Memories of Henry soon faded after his death, when his achievements were eclipsed by those of his illustrious son, Henry V, in whose reign

Henry IV as drawn in Cassell's *History of England*. In 1403 Henry was 36 years old and still in peak physical condition. In his later reign, Henry suffered repeated bouts of ill health, believed by some contemporaries to be a divine punishment for the execution of Richard Scrope, archbishop of York. (Author's collection)

HENRY IV.

The tournament at St Inglevert was a famous event described in detail in Froissart's *Chronicles*. Henry of Bolingbroke and Hotspur both attended the tourney with other English knights and men-at-arms. (British Library, Ms. Harley 4379, f. 43)

England achieved unimaginable victories against the French. Henry IV has therefore been relegated to the second rank among English kings. It is telling that Shakespeare, in his play *Henry IV, Part I*, chose to cast Prince Hal in the leading, coming-of-age hero role rather than his more problematic father. Recent biographies, however, have stressed the achievements of Henry's reign and career up to 1399.

Born in 1367 to John of Gaunt, duke of Lancaster, Henry became the heir to the greatest inheritance of medieval England, with wealth and landholdings second only to the king. In April 1377 Henry, as earl of Derby, attended Edward III's last Garter day celebration and was knighted by his grandfather, alongside Prince Richard and Hotspur. Henry soon developed an avid interest in the traditional martial pursuits pursued by young members of the nobility, becoming particularly skilful at jousting. In his first household account, dating from October 1381 to September 1382, Henry, aged only 14 or 15, can be shown to have participated in at least three jousts over the course of the year. The first followed the royal wedding of Richard II and Anne of Bohemia, for which event Henry's accounts record the purchase of 1000 gilded copper sequins to decorate himself and his mount. Throughout Henry's early life, his participation in the jousts was a common occurrence and he gained a considerable degree of fame and acknowledgement for his exploits. This was not a frivolous pastime. The art of jousting was a great test of military skill and drew attention to Henry as a potential war leader. The pursuit also required a high degree of confidence and self-assurance, both qualities required of a successful knight. The most famous joust Henry attended was that held at St Inglevert, near Calais, in the spring of 1390. Three French knights sent out a formal challenge inviting all comers to ride against them, attracting 105 English men-at-arms to take up the challenge.

The Great Seal of England was used to authenticate documents with the approval of the king. On the obverse of the seal, Henry IV is shown as a lawgiver sat in judgement, replete with the regalia and symbols of kingship. On the reverse, Henry is depicted as a mounted knight ready to defend his kingdom and uphold justice through feats of arms. (Author's collection)

Henry travelled with a retinue of Lancastrian retainers and the sons of the nobility, with Hotspur among his most notable companions. The two were similar in age and his presence in Henry's retinue raises the possibility of a friendship based upon their shared enthusiasm for chivalric pursuits. At the jousts, Henry rode five lances down the lists against each of his French counterparts and was singled out for praise for his skill and largesse by the monk of Saint-Denys, the French royal chronicler.

Not all of Henry's military effort was expended on tournaments. In 1387, his part in the battle of Radcot Bridge was given by some chroniclers as a critical factor in the Appellants' easy victory over Robert de Vere, earl of Oxford. From August 1390 to March 1391, Henry participated in the crusade taking place between the Teutonic Order and the pagan inhabitants of the kingdom of Lithuania. Henry was present at the unsuccessful siege of Vilnius but, in contrast to the failure of the campaign, managed to earn international recognition for his feats. The Prussian chronicler, John von Posilge, praised him for fighting manfully throughout the war, while his English retinue also received acclaim for capturing an important outlying fort during the siege and raising their banner over the ramparts, while their Prussian and Livonian allies stood idly by.

In 1392 Henry returned to Prussia only to find that peace had broken out. Instead of the planned crusade, Henry determined on a pilgrimage to the Holy Land, travelling through Prague, Vienna and Venice before setting sail for Jaffa in December, stopping during the voyage at Corfu and Rhodes. Travelling to Jerusalem, he spent ten days in the area, visiting the Holy Sepulchre and other sites before returning to England, reaching London in July 1393. During his journey, Henry had met, and been entertained by, some of Europe's most prestigious princes, including Wenceslaus, king of the Romans, Sigismund, king of Hungary, Albert, duke of Austria and Gian Galeazzo Visconti, later duke of Milan. On the way he had also acquired a growing menagerie, comprising an ostrich, a parrot and a leopard, which was furnished with its own cabin on the sea-journeys to and from the Holy Land.

Henry's birth and experiences had earned him a place amongst the elite of Europe's nobility. However, the events of 1399 seriously harmed his reputation and many, particularly among those who had benefited during Richard II's reign, were not prepared to be easily reconciled to his rule, despite his unarguable personal qualities. The spectre of Richard continued to haunt Henry throughout his reign, and in 1403 the lustre of his previous achievements had been severely tarnished. Nevertheless, at 36 years old, Henry remained at the peak of his physical powers, while the large Lancastrian affinity developed by him and his father ensured Henry substantial military support.

Henry, prince of Wales, better known to history as Henry V, victor of Agincourt, was born in Monmouth on 16 September 1386. Aged 12 when his father was exiled, the young Henry seems to have developed an affectionate relationship with Richard II, with

Prince Henry receiving a copy of Hoccleve's *Regiment of Princes* from an unknown kneeling figure, possibly the author. The prince is often supposed to have led a riotous life during his youth but proved a capable commander during his military apprenticeship in Wales. (British Library, Ms. Arundel 38, f. 37)

whom he travelled to Ireland on campaign in 1399. At news of Bolingbroke's return, the young Henry remained in Ireland in honourable captivity. At his father's coronation, Henry was created the prince of Wales, duke of Cornwall and Aquitaine, earl of Chester, and on 10 November, gained the title (but not the land) of duke of Lancaster. The prince shared the early dangers of Henry IV's early reign with his father and soon began to shoulder his share of the military duties and problems facing the Lancastrian regime. Principal among these burdens was Owain Glyndŵr's revolt, which soon came to threaten Prince Henry's main source of patrimony and income. Travelling to the country in which he would spend much of the next decade campaigning, Henry spent time under the tutelage of Hotspur, learning the tactics of Welsh and border warfare. In 1401 the prince was present at the siege of Conwy, which had been taken in a surprise attack by the Welsh while the English were observing a religious service in the town. Percy influence continued when Thomas Percy, earl of Worcester, was appointed as his governor and advisor in November 1401. In 1402, Henry had his first major military success when he led an English march to resupply the castles at Harlech and Conwy. This was especially commendable as two other divisions led by more experienced commanders, including the king and the earls of Stafford and Warwick, were hampered by bad weather and forced into an embarrassing and ignominious retreat. During this campaign, the king himself came close to death when his tent blew down in a storm, but was propitiously saved by going to sleep in his armour, preventing him from being crushed.

In April 1403 Henry was granted more independent command, perhaps in recognition of his previous success. He was made royal lieutenant for the whole of Wales, with a substantial force under his command. By the battle of Shrewsbury, therefore, Henry was an increasingly experienced and aware military commander, being in the midst of a strenuous military apprenticeship in Wales. The riotous youth Henry is occasionally supposed to have enjoyed was, instead, largely a tutelage in the difficulties of fighting against a Welsh guerrilla campaign with only limited financial resources at his disposal.

Edmund, earl of Stafford, inherited his earldom in April 1395. His eldest brother had been murdered by Richard II's half-brother, John Holland, during a brawl in the Scottish campaign of 1385. Richard's reluctance to punish Holland sufficiently may have persuaded Edmund to support Henry IV in 1399. Made a Knight of the Bath and Knight of the Garter by Henry IV, Stafford was also raised to the office of Constable of England on the eve of the battle.

The Scottish **George Dunbar, earl of March,** was one of the most important assets Henry IV possessed. His military record was exemplary and despite his age (he was born *c.*1336/8), he was active in the border warfare of the early 1400s. He was the victor of the battle of Nesbit Moor in 1402, and was credited with devising the battle plan that led to the Percys' success at the battle of Homildon Hill. In spring 1402, he was involved in the siege of Cocklaw but his competing interest on the border with the Percys and the earl of Douglas led him to favour Henry IV during the Shrewsbury campaign.

The earl of Stafford depicted in a mid-15th century manuscript known as *Sir Thomas Holme's Book of Arms* (British Library, Ms. Harley 4205, f. 73)

The soldier and chronicler Jean de Waurin provides us with a list of important lords who fought for Henry IV at Shrewsbury not included by other chroniclers. His account of the battle, however, is problematic, confused and requires careful scrutiny. Within Henry's army he lists three dukes: York (identified as Henry's uncle), Gloucester and Surrey; four earls: Arundel, Rutland, Exeter and Somerset and additionally, the Lord de Ros. Some of these names are clearly mistaken. Henry's uncle Edmund, duke of York, had died in 1402, with his eldest son Edward gaining the title. Edward's own earldom of Rutland was subsequently in abeyance at the time of Shrewsbury. However, as

The Lords Appellant, including Henry of Bolingbroke (second from right), stand in front of Richard II. Two of the most prominent nobles who fought for Henry IV at Shrewsbury, Thomas FitzAlan and Richard Beauchamp, were sons of former Appellants. (Author's collection)

Edward and his brother, Richard of Conisbrough, served in Wales and the Welsh borders in 1403, it is possible that both were at the battle. Additionally problematic, the duchies of Gloucester and Surrey were similarly in abeyance at the date of the battle. The king's fourth son, Humphrey, became duke of Gloucester only in 1414 and, at 12 years of age, is unlikely to have taken an active part in any fighting. The inclusion of the duke of Surrey as a participant is likewise hard to understand. The last duke of Surrey, Thomas Holland, had forfeited his duchy in 1399 and was executed for his part in the Epiphany Rising in 1400. Furthermore, the earldoms of Surrey and Arundel were in the possession of a single individual, Thomas FitzAlan.

In de Waurin's list, however, he clearly treats the two titles as belonging to separate individuals. He has the 'young' duke of Surrey leading the rearguard while the earl of Arundel stood with the king. While FitzAlan can be confidently placed within the battle by other sources, it is uncertain to whom else Waurin could be referring. The most likely individual is Edmund Holland, earl of Kent, (younger brother of Thomas Holland, mentioned above) to whom Wavrin may have mistakenly attributed his brother's forfeited titles. Importantly, both Edmund and another of Waurin's inclusions, William de Ros, 6th baron de Ros, were created Knights of the Garter soon after the battle, most likely as a reward for their participation, while de Ros additionally served as Lord Treasurer of England in 1403–04. Happily, the earls of Exeter and Somerset can be more positively identified as Henry's half-brothers, John and Thomas Beaufort. John had been created earl and marquis of Somerset in 1397 while Thomas was elevated to the duchy of Exeter in 1416. Both had interests in the March, John as lieutenant of South Wales and Thomas as constable of Ludlow.

In addition to the named and possible members of the nobility, numerous lesser knights and gentry were present in the royal army fighting for Henry IV. Many of those listed in the chronicles had strong Lancastrian backgrounds with numerous years of service for Henry IV and his father, John of Gaunt. The most prominent within the sources is **Walter Blount** of Derbyshire, king's knight, who had been a strong Lancastrian supporter since his service with John of Gaunt in Spain in 1367. Blount's Spanish wife was one of the ladies in attendance to Gaunt's wife, Constanza of Castile, and he was also among the first to join Bolingbroke when he landed at Ravenspur in 1399.

OPPOSING FORCES

REBEL FORCES

English archers had been highly effective in **numerous** English battles against the French, such as Sluys (1340), Crécy (1346) and Poitiers (1356). Among the most accomplished archers were those from Cheshire, who were used in successive English campaigns in Wales and France. This picture shows archers of the late 14th century in a copy of Jean Cuvelier's *La chanson de Bertrand du Guesclin* (British Library, Ms. Yates Thompson 35, f. 51)

The rebellion against Henry IV in the summer of 1403 was foremost a Cheshire affair. Although instigated and led by men from the north, all the evidence suggests that the greater part of the rebel army was levied in the county palatine. Cheshire had a recent history of discontent with the new Lancastrian government. During the Epiphany Rising of 1400, two Lancashire squires, John and Adam Hesketh, were dispatched to Cheshire to inform the people that the earls of Salisbury and Kent had put Henry IV to flight and forced him into refuge within the Tower of London. Richard II's supporters were called upon to muster at Shrewsbury on 14 January, to restore the deposed king, then still alive in Henry's captivity, by force. Among the targets for the rebels was Chester Castle that, for two days, was in danger of being taken, until news of the failure of the rising was heard and the participants decided to disperse. The seriousness of this abortive rising was not lost on the new regime and an inquiry, led by Hotspur, was soon established. A general pardon was issued by Henry IV in May 1400, from which 125 prominent men were specifically excluded and required to sue for individual pardons.

The primary reason for Cheshire's discontent was its long established and close connection with Richard II. During his reign, Richard had assiduously cultivated the county, most prominently promoting Cheshire into a palatinate under direct royal rule. Many Cheshiremen were also called upon by Richard for military service, especially during his ill-fated Scottish campaign of 1385 and Irish expeditions of 1394 and 1399. During the latter, the *Dieulacres Chronicle* records that the captains of his personal bodyguard consisted of 'seven warlike and worthy squires' from Cheshire: John Legh of Booths; Richard Cholmely; Ralph Davenport; Adam Bostok; John Downe; Thomas Beston and Thomas Holford. These men wore Richard's personal livery badge of the white hart on their shoulders in a prominent display of their royal association. Most took part in the rising of 1400, and all but Davenport would later fight against Henry IV at Shrewsbury.

The association between Richard and Cheshire had gone back at least as far as the battle of Radcot Bridge between the Appellants and forces loyal to the king. The royalist army under Robert de Vere, duke of Ireland, was comprised mostly of Cheshiremen, some of whom Richard later rewarded with 4,000 marks for their loyalty and participation. The relationship between Richard and the region may have been a continuation of the policy begun by his father, Edward the Black Prince. Cheshiremen served under Edward at the battles of Crécy, Poitiers and Nájera, and were often employed as garrison and household soldiers abroad. In 1355, when the Black Prince was made lieutenant of Gascony, Cheshiremen are known to have joined him, arrayed in hats and tunics coloured green and white.

Cheshire archers

One of the main reasons behind the recruitment of Cheshiremen in royal campaigns seems to have been the particularly high quality of its fighting men. In the later Middle Ages, Cheshire probably saw a higher proportion of its population recruited into English armies than any other county. This was partly in relation to the Welsh campaigns of successive English monarchs, but it was also an important acknowledgement of their skill and ferocity in battle. A late 14th-century chronicler claimed that 'because of former wars and disputes among themselves they are better trained in arms, and more difficult to control than other people in the kingdom'. Practice and skill in the use of the longbow seems to have been a particular talent. In 1277, a corps of specialized archers was levied from Macclesfield for Edward I's first Welsh War. In 1298 Edward again made use of Cheshire archers, and at the battle of Falkirk they fully proved their worth by decimating the Scottish schiltrons. In 1334, Cheshiremen were specially chosen by Edward III to form an elite band of 200 mounted king's archers.

Richard II expanded the association between the Crown and Cheshire archers when he chose them to form a personal bodyguard loyal only to himself. In July 1397, Richard ordered the sheriff of Chester to muster 2000 archers for royal service, who were employed during the trial of the Lords Appellant. During the proceedings they were a constant menace to all present, at one point shooting their arrows 'to the terror of everyone'. Richard later retained 760 of these men, who travelled with the king wearing his livery. As time went by, these Cheshire archers gained a particularly sinister reputation. According to Walsingham, they were 'by nature bestial, ready to commit every sort of crime, respecting neither rank nor wealth'. So great did their unruliness become 'that before long, when travelling through the realm with the king, either within the royal household or apart from it, they began to beat and wound with impunity the king's faithful subjects; some indeed, with extraordinary cruelty, they killed. They also seized people's goods, paying nothing for their provisions, and raped and ravished both married and unmarried women, for no one dared to stand up to them.'

Several sources also record that they were hated by the rest of Richard's household for their over-familiarity with the king. John Strecche of Kenilworth records that they frequently referred to him as 'Dycun', an informal and intimate diminutive of the name Richard: 'Dycun [Dickon] sleep securely while we wake and fear not whilst we live.' The loyalty of these men, despite their lack of propriety, was firmly established and Richard's memory continued to inspire devotion amongst them, even after his death.

As firm anti-Lancastrians it was natural that many of the archers joined Hotspur's rebellion. Despite their poor reputation, they remained formidable soldiers, far outmatching those Henry IV could muster. Even hostile chroniclers did not underestimate their ability, and Walsingham begrudgingly praises those at Shrewsbury as 'the pick of the county of Chester'. There is also evidence to suggest that on campaign the archers served with professionalism, contrary to their evil reputation. John Hardyng, fighting alongside them in Hotspur's army, recorded that they were 'fyne withouten Raskaldry'. All the other accounts that mention them suggest that the Cheshire archers were an invaluable asset to Hotspur.

Cheshire gentry

Richard II heavily relied on the Cheshire gentry and rewarded many with office and positions of rank within the county and the realm. When Henry IV came to the throne, the loyalty of such men was suspect and the new regime often sought to replace them with those claiming a strong history of Lancastrian service. To the local gentry, access to royal patronage and regional office was a fundamental source of maintaining social standing, wealth and power. Supporters of Richard now found these avenues of advancement blocked. Prominent among the excluded were members of Richard's bodyguard while, in some cases, entire families were forced into the political wilderness. In 1399, John Legh of Booths served as the leader of the king's guard, Sir Hugh Legh as escheator, Sir Robert Legh as sheriff of the county and Peter Legh as steward of Macclesfield. In 1403 none of these men remained in their previous positions or held administrative power within the county. Such men naturally looked towards Hotspur as a means of restoring the losses sustained following the deposition of Richard II. Hotspur was clever to manipulate these grievances and, in the proclamation declaring the beginning of the revolt, was careful to ask only for the loyalty that the Cheshiremen had shown the former king. This may also have been intended to dupe those who were still hopeful that Richard was still alive. In the early 1400s, stories of Richard's survival were commonplace, most prominently when the Scots disseminated a rumour to this end during the winter of 1401–02. They found an imposter by the name of Thomas Ward of Trumpington to impersonate the king and sightings of Richard were reported in Berwick, Wales and Westminster – causing even Charles VI of France to dispatch the historian Jean Creton to report on the rumours. Hopes of Richard's survival were therefore strong and it would be a mistake to think that all members of the gentry, still less the lower ranks, were informed enough not to believe the rumours.

Ties of kinship and familial allegiance were an important consideration in deciding which side to support. Detailed study of the individuals involved in the rebellion reveals a close network of interdependence and local interests that encouraged men to take up arms. For example, Richard Bromley, who fought against Henry IV, can be identified as a neighbour of the Leghs of Booths while another rebel, William Legh of Baguley, was a more distant member of the family. Other prominent rebels no doubt had a large influence on their fellow members of the gentry. Sir John Mascy of Tatton and Sir Peter Dutton were neighbours in the Hundred of Bucklow and were key figures, along with the Leghs, in promoting the rising in this area. A particular figure likely to have been influenced by Massey was the esquire Peter Warburton, whose conflicting loyalties in 1403 demonstrate clearly the difficulty faced by many among the Cheshire gentry in deciding which side to support. Warburton was a tenant in the Lancastrian lordship of Halton and had a history of service for the Lancastrians, having served in Bolingbroke's household during the year 1398. Despite this background, Warburton preferred service with Hotspur at Shrewsbury, presumably influenced by the long-standing association between him and Sir John Mascy of Tatton, his former guardian and whose daughter he had formerly been contracted to marry.

Another factor that may have swayed members of the Cheshire gentry was service under Hotspur and the earl of Worcester in the years 1399–1403. Both had been frequently present in the region following Henry IV's usurpation and had often served on campaign with members of the Cheshire gentry, allowing them to build personal followings among the important men of the county. This probably does much to explain the defections of Sir Hugh Browe, Sir William Stanley and Sir John Pulle, alongside Worcester, from Prince Henry's Shrewsbury garrison. Stanley and Pulle, for example, had been retained by Hotspur to relieve Beaumaris in 1402, while Browe had been with Hotspur on campaign in 1401. Unlike the Leghs, these men had not been estranged from sources of royal patronage. Stanley, for instance, was a family member of Sir John Stanley, steward of the prince's household, and therefore had reason to expect the possibility of further preferment and reward. It is possible that factors such as Hotspur's reputation, force of personality and recent military success at the battle of Homildon Hill persuaded such men that the Percys had a realistic chance of emerging victorious.

Hotspur's readiness to meet the costs of his soldiers out of his own pocket during the Welsh campaigns may also have been influential, especially as it contrasted so favourably with Prince Henry's own inability to pay his men, funded as he was largely by royal revenue. In September 1400 and again in 1401, the *Dieulacres Chronicle* mentions that there were high numbers of desertions from the English army. In 1403 many of the Cheshire gentry failed to attend an assembly at which the council's proposals for another expedition in North Wales were to be presented. This was symptomatic of the dissatisfaction felt towards Henry IV, his policies and the Lancastrian government.

Other participants

One important factor governing the recruitment of Hotspur's army was the route it took towards Shrewsbury. The rising seems to have begun within the Hundred of Bucklow, probably as this was where Hotspur first entered the county. The Macclesfield and Northwich Hundreds were also important early areas of recruitment, with Eddisbury and Broxton providing men soon afterwards. Many men also appear to have joined the rebellion from Wales, most likely due to Hotspur's service in the area. This rising was also

Many among the Cheshire gentry benefited during Richard II's reign and remained loyal to his memory after his death in 1400. In this manuscript illumination, Richard can be seen with his men-at-arms in Ireland, knighting Henry of Monmouth, soon to become Prince Henry. (British Library, Ms. Yates Thompson 35, f. 51)

encouraged by certain members of the clergy, whose names are recorded in later documents as having arrived in arms with their parishioners to the battle. These included the parsons of Rousthorne, Hawardyn, Pulforde, Dodleston, Hanley and Davenham.

When such incitement failed, the rebels had no compunction about employing coercion. John Kynaston, Steward of Lord Lestrange in the Hundred of Ellesmere, pressed the local tenants into service under the pretence of fighting for the king. Upon reaching the village of Myddle, the tenants wished to return home as Lord Lestrange had not joined them in person. Kynaston responded by threatening to hang, draw and behead any who did not follow him. Upon reaching the rebel army, the tenants were forced into armed service against their will. It is likely that many low-born individuals were conscripted in a similar fashion among both armies.

ROYAL FORCES

The recruitment of Henry IV's army for the Shrewsbury campaign was directly in response to news of the rising and conducted in a hurried manner. It is clear that the full extent of the immediate danger did not become apparent until five days before the battle on 16 July 1403, upon which date he sent a mandate from Burton upon Trent to the sheriffs of all adjoining counties – Oxfordshire, Berkshire, Bedfordshire, Buckinghamshire, Warwickshire, Leicestershire, Northamptonshire, Nottinghamshire, Staffordshire, Derbyshire, Lincolnshire and Rutland – to collect their forces and come to his assistance as quickly as possible. Before reaching Burton, Henry had been heading north in anticipation of fighting with the Percys against the Scots. The size of his retinue at this stage is unknown but can be estimated from other sources. A document dated 17 July lists payments to a force consisting of four barons, 20 knights, 476 esquires and 2500 archers. Although this would infer that Henry already possessed a sizeable force, it has been suggested that this payment refers instead to an earlier and unrelated campaign. In April 1405, in response to Archbishop Scrope's rebellion, Henry is known to have travelled with 144 men-at-arms and 720 archers. This would seem to be a far more credible indication of his fighting numbers at the commencement of the Shrewsbury campaign. This modest force would, however, have been bolstered by the smaller retinues of the accompanying nobility. The days from the 16th to the 21st must have been a period of intense recruitment, and all indications suggest that Henry's call was highly effective, despite the short time available. Some indication of areas which responded is provided by the tomb monuments of those killed during the battle. Unsurprisingly, these are located within a short distance of the route taken by Henry on his march towards Shrewsbury. For example, Sir Robert Mavesyn of Mavesyn Ridware, near Rugeley, probably joined the king as he marched from Burton to Stafford. Sir Thomas Wendesley and Sir Edmund Cockayne were

Sir Edmund Cockayne was killed fighting for Henry IV at Shrewsbury. His effigy lies in the Boothby Chapel of St Oswald's Church in Ashbourne, Derbyshire. (Author's photograph)

also in an excellent position to join the king from their estates in Derbyshire. These knights also emphasize the way in which Henry was able to rely on the Lancastrian affinity developed by John of Gaunt. Edmund Cockayne's father John had served as steward of the household to Gaunt while Wendesley had served in Gaunt's retinue as an esquire. Upon the duke's death, the loyalty of such men transferred over to his son and, in 1399, Wendesley was one of the Derbyshire knights who rallied to Henry after his return to England, for which service he was rewarded with the large sum of £60. When summoned in 1403, he again responded, although by this date he was already over 60 years old. Another Lancastrian retainer, Sir John Luttrell, whom Henry had made a knight of the Bath in 1399, received Henry's summons in Somerset and hastily made a will, declaring that he was 'going with all possible speed to join his most dread lord the king … to resist the malice of the false traitor Sir Henry Percy'.

One of the most interesting points about the battle is that not all of the Cheshiremen involved fought on a single side. Those who had benefited from Lancastrian policies in the palatinate had reason to continue supporting Henry IV and the majority of such men remained loyal, despite the anti-Lancastrian feelings of many in the county. The king's retinue at Shrewsbury included the mayor of Chester, the attorney-general of the county, the constable of Cheshire Castle and the prince's lieutenant in Cheshire and Flintshire. Henry also had his own connections within the county, such as in his lordship of Halton, which continued to provide soldiers throughout his reign. Another supporter of Henry at Shrewsbury, Sir John Mascy of Puddington, demonstrated the limited success of Lancastrian policy in attracting Cheshiremen to his cause. Mascy had served Henry during the Scottish campaign in the summer of 1400, bringing with him 60 men at arms and 500 archers. His later service, however, had been less favourable as it had been he who had been most implicated in the loss of Conwy Castle to the Welsh in 1401. For their loyalty there is evidence that the properties of such men were specifically targeted for revenge by fellow Cheshiremen and several houses in Nantwich were burned to the ground.

The tomb of Sir Thomas Wendesley in All Saint's Church, Bakewell, Derbyshire, features a bascinet inscribed with the words 'IHC NAZAREN', an abbreviated version of 'Jesus Christ the Nazarene'. This was a common invocation and may have been thought to offer the wearer a degree of protection, as well as being a badge of his Christian virtue and faith. (Author's photograph)

NUMBERS

Estimating the numbers involved in medieval battles is notoriously difficult and Shrewsbury is no exception. Almost all the sources agree that the royal army was larger than the rebel side, though most sources wildly exaggerate the total numbers involved. Jean de Waurin and the *Dieulacres Chronicle* provide the fantastical figure of 60,000 in the royal army, while the latter credits Hotspur with only 7,000 men. The contemporary Scottish chronicler Andrew Wyntoun suggests a more reasonable balance between the two armies, but his numbers remain too high at 30,000 and 20,000 apiece. Walsingham provides the most sensible estimate of 14,000 in the royal army and 10,000 in the rebel ranks. Modern historians, however, have argued that the short time available for recruitment probably meant that both armies were, in fact, rather smaller than the figures provided, even by Walsingham.

OPPOSING PLANS

THE PERCYS

Hotspur's marriage to Elizabeth Mortimer united the two most powerful houses of the Scottish and Welsh borders. Hotspur's desire to ransom his brother-in-law Edmund Mortimer caused difficulties between him and Henry IV. This mid-15th-century drawing shows two men-at-arms in Mortimer and Percy heraldry. (British Library, Ms. Harley 4205, f. 45 & f. 50)

Contrary to Percy hopes, Henry IV had proved by 1403 that he was unwilling to be easily dominated by the will of his subjects. The determination of the king to follow his own policies often meant that royal decisions were taken without deference, and in occasional opposition to the political and territorial aspirations of the Percy family. Symptomatic of Henry's refusal to be persuaded by Percy desires were his refusal to pay the Percys more than he thought they were owed and the simultaneous favours shown to Ralph Neville and George Dunbar. These advancements were also indicative of Henry's growing confidence in his position on the throne and his decreased reliance on his principle adherents during the events of 1399. Although the new political landscape may not have actively threatened the pre-eminent position the Percys had gained in the border counties, it nevertheless demonstrated that they would no longer be able to rely on the king's favour.

It also appears that the proximity to power enjoyed by the Percys after 1399 had a profound effect on their ambitions and notions of their own grandeur. Several contemporary chronicles contain clues suggesting that they desired control of the Crown, and there were even suspicions that they coveted it for themselves. After their victory against the Scots at Homildon Hill, the contemporary Welsh lawyer and chronicler Adam Usk writes that they became haughty and 'too much puffed up'. In the letter sent to Henry IV on 26 June 1403, the earl of Northumberland signed the document as 'Your Mathathias' – a biblical allusion, perhaps designed to remind Henry that his seizure of the Crown was indebted to Percy support. The Percys' role as kingmakers to Henry IV had provided the family with previously unobtainable power and influence. The temptation was therefore strong to repeat the action, except this time with an eye to establishing themselves as the power behind the throne in a more secure and enduring settlement. Hotspur's 11-year-old nephew, the earl of March, had a strong claim to the throne to rival that of Henry IV. If the Percys could place March on the throne, their control of government for the considerable future would seemingly be assured. According to the contemporary chronicle the *Incerti scriptoris Chronicon Angliae*, Thomas Percy desired Henry IV's death 'so that he might be better governed under his kinsman'. Like Hotspur and Northumberland, Thomas Percy may have felt that the Percy star was beginning to wane. Although entrusted with an array of duties between 1399 and 1402, he had since lost his position of steward of the household and the lieutenancy of Wales.

Another possibility is that the Percys began the rebellion to take the crown for themselves. According to the *Dieulacres Chronicle*, Henry IV accused Hotspur of holding this desire in the negotiations before the battle. Reports of Percy soldiers shouting 'Henry Percy King!' at Shrewsbury also make this prospect more than idle speculation.

The Percy shield of arms in the mid-15th-century manuscript British Library Royal 18 D II is surrounded by the insignia of the order of the Garter. All three of the Percys had been created knights of the Garter: Northumberland in 1366; Thomas in 1376; and Hotspur in 1388. (British Library, Ms. Royal 18 D II, f. 162)

If the Percys wanted to remove Henry IV, they had to do so by force of arms. The family's successful war record from 1399 to 1403 stood in stark contrast to the military failures of Henry IV. The royal campaign in Scotland in the summer of 1400 had failed to produce any significant achievements, despite costing the exchequer the huge sum of £10,000. The Percy success at Homildon Hill, looked upon with jealousy by the king, was therefore an issue of some contention between them, a matter that Henry IV did nothing to improve in his uncompromising attitude towards the Scottish prisoners. In Wales, Glyndŵr's revolt also continued to threaten effective English rule in the principality and Henry's efforts there had ended in similar failure. For these reasons, the Percys may have believed themselves to be more than a match for the king in terms of military strength and ability.

The level of prior consideration and planning done by the Percys is uncertain. The confusion is evident in the sources that offer conflicting accounts of their intentions, as well as the reasons behind the revolt and the culpability of different members of the family. It cannot be doubted, however, that the main intention of the rebellion was to remove Henry IV and the Lancastrian regime from power. That the Percys had not miscalculated their own strength is evidenced by the fact that the rising immediately escalated into the most significant threat faced by Henry during his reign.

OWAIN GLYNDŴR

By 1403 Glyndŵr had proved that his revolt was not going to be easily defeated. The Welsh had achieved victories at the battles of Mynydd Hyddgen in 1401 and Pilleth in 1402, as well as securing more modest successes such as the surprise capture of Conwy Castle in 1401 and the capture of Glyndŵr's arch enemy, Reginald Grey, Lord Ruthin, in 1402. While impressive and heavily disruptive to the English administration, these accomplishments were relatively small scale and did not represent a significant threat to English hegemony in the principality. In 1403, however, the revolt became truly national. A significant campaign was planned by Glyndŵr for the summer, in which a victory over the English would increase his prestige and legitimize his claims to be the rightful prince of Wales.

HENRY IV

Although Henry IV was well aware of the worsening relations between himself and the Percy family, the revolt came suddenly and unexpectedly. Apart from the story of the physical confrontation between Hotspur and the king contained in the *Brut*, there is no record of any active hostility on the part of the Lancastrian government. As far as the king was concerned, the Percys were his most powerful subjects, important to the defence of his kingdom and, while Henry had occasionally rewarded their local rivals, this had not substantially altered Percy fortunes. There is also plentiful evidence that Henry desired to keep the Percys content. When Hotspur kept custody of the earl of Douglas, in contravention of Henry's requests, the king declined to press the issue, despite his evident displeasure. The Scottish grant was also clearly designed to allow the Percys to fulfil their long-held ambitions. Although Henry could not satisfy the Percys' monetary requirements, his commitment to the cause of securing English domination of the border is demonstrated by the fact that in June 1403 he was preparing to move north in support of the Percys. When news of the rebellion reached him, the king was therefore taken completely by surprise – so much so that he seems at first to have doubted the early reports. However, once the irrefutable fact of the revolt had been impressed upon him, his immediate plans shifted to his own defence and that of the realm.

Henry IV wearing a crown and holding a sceptre, the two most potent symbols of medieval kingship. Although Henry had survived danger to his own person during the Epiphany Rising in 1400, the Percy rebellion was a far more serious and unexpected threat to his rule. (British Library, Ms. Harley 4205, f. 7)

THE CAMPAIGN

HOTSPUR'S MOVEMENTS

Sometime in the first week of July, Hotspur came south from Cocklaw with the earl of Douglas and a small band of adherents. This included two of his esquires, Thomas Knayton and Roger Salvayn, his personal chaplain, John Ambell, and a few other men of the 'far north', including the chronicler John Hardyng. Other than Douglas, it seems that the members of this group were all close personal associates of Hotspur, with a history of service and reward to and from the Percy family. Knayton, for example, had been given the constableship of Bamburgh Castle by Hotspur and owed his rise to Percy patronage. In addition to these select men, the chronicler Edward Hall notes that Percy came south with 'other erles of Scotland with a greate armie'. It appears, however, that this claim is mistaken. Hotspur's initial strategy relied on speed and ensuring his sudden movements remained concealed from Henry IV, neither of which objectives could have been achieved with a substantial Scottish force. According to the author of the *Dieulacres Chronicle*, Hotspur achieved this secrecy by travelling through Lancashire feigning peace. Any deception was no doubt facilitated by Hotspur's frequent presence in the

The inner bailey of Chester Castle in a watercolour painted in 1750 by Moses Griffith. The Castle was besieged by forces loyal to Richard II in 1399 and was used by as a base by Hotspur in 1403. (Grosvenor Museum)

region in the preceding years and the numerous legitimate reasons he had to visit, occasioned by the offices and property he still held in Cheshire and north Wales. In these circumstances, it is unlikely that his sudden arrival in the north-west would have aroused undue suspicion. It was only the presence of Douglas that might have been expected to raise awkward questions, but these could easily be beaten off by Hotspur maintaining the pretence that Douglas remained his prisoner.

The exact route taken from Cocklaw to Cheshire is unknown, as the *Dieulacres Chronicle* only mentions in passing that the group came 'through parts of Lancashire'. Given that Hotspur did not recruit heavily outside Cheshire, it is likely that the fastest route possible was taken, past Lancaster on the western side of the Pennines. As Hotspur neared his destination he began to make the first steps to assemble an army and recruited several members of the Lancashire gentry into his small retinue. These included Sir Gilbert Halsall of Halsall, near Southport, Thomas Bradshaw of Haigh, near Wigan, and Geoffrey Bold, who held the manors of Lower Darwen and Whittleswick, near Eccles.

Hotspur arrived at Chester on 9 July. There he was entertained at the house of Petronilla Clerk, mother of John Kyngesley, an esquire from Nantwich who had received a life annuity from Richard II in 1397. Once in the city, Hotspur wasted no time in raising an army. To agitate the population to rebellion, he released a proclamation that Richard II was still alive, both in Chester and throughout the market towns of Cheshire. Those who desired to see the former king were directed to assemble on St Kenelm's feast day (17 July) 'beyond the forest of Delamere at Sandiway, at the sixth hour'. This gap between Hotspur's arrival and the planned muster gave ample time for potential allies to join the rebellion. It is likely that Hotspur and his small retinue spent the intervening 12 days in a flurry of activity, organizing and recruiting men amenable to the rising. However, if the delay gave Hotspur the chance to recruit a sizeable army so, too, did it give time for Henry IV to receive news of events in Cheshire. Declaring open rebellion at this point, therefore, without the guarantee of extensive armed support, constituted a considerable risk. Although familiar with the county and most of the leading gentry, Hotspur cannot have known before his proclamation how successful his attempts would prove. Fortunately for the rebellion, his calculated gamble proved correct and succeeded in provoking a substantial resurgence in anti-Lancastrian, pro-Ricardian sentiment throughout the county. In the words of Walsingham: 'though [Hotspur's words] were false, they stirred differing emotions in the hearts of many people … for there were many who felt some affection for King Richard … especially those who formerly had been his household servants [or] had been granted fiefs by him or had received other gifts. Others, while not openly declaring for the rebels were forced to waver not sure which party it was safer to support.'

In addition to his other public proclamations, Hotspur promised that there would be a large army under the earl of Northumberland waiting to meet those attending the muster at Sandiway. Whether this was a true intention, or a deliberate falsehood designed to fool a greater number into joining the rebellion, is unclear. Unfortunately, other than his location in Yorkshire, Northumberland's actions and motivations at this stage are subject to debate. According to Edward Hall, Northumberland was taken ill when Hotspur came south, but promised to rendezvous with his son once the

The city of Shrewsbury lies within a naturally defensive position within a bend of the river Severn. The castle defended the entrance to the city and can be seen to the left of the railway bridge, near the centre of the photograph. (© Ian Bracegirdle Aerial Photography)

sickness had passed. Hardyng, however, gives no indication that the rebels in Cheshire had any knowledge of Northumberland's malady, scorning the earl for failing his son 'foully without thought or reason'.

It is possible that Northumberland had intended to support his son in Cheshire and that illness did serve to prevent his arrival. Another potential reason, however, is that Northumberland had always intended to stay in the north gathering support and waiting for news of Henry IV's reaction. The plan could then have been to converge on the king with two separate armies. Another, more remote, possibility is that Northumberland was in disagreement with Hotspur and had not been involved in the plan. This was indeed Northumberland's later claim and was thought credible by contemporaries. Instead of marching towards Shrewsbury to join Hotspur, he said, he was attempting to promote peace.

Whatever the true nature of the plan, the possibility of extensive armed assistance must have re-assured Cheshiremen previously unsure of supporting the rebellion. According to the author of the *Dieulacres Chronicle*, a 'multitude of fools of both sexes' arrived at Sandiway on the strength of Hotspur's promises. Once assembled, however, the pretence of Richard's survival and the imminent arrival of Northumberland and his army could not be maintained. Instead, according to The *English Chronicle*, Hotspur appeared before them at the head of a band of 'strong and warlike' men, wearing Richard II's livery of a white hart. He then addressed the crowd, lamenting his role in Richard's deposition, lambasting the poor government of Henry IV and promising to amend the situation if he could. By a mixture of such promises and pre-existing disaffection towards the Lancastrian regime, men soon began to join his army. Other participants, having come to Sandiway out of little more than curiosity, found themselves forcibly conscripted.

Leaving Sandiway, Hotspur had several directions in which he could march his newly assembled army. One possible course was to make a direct assault on the Lancastrian government by marching towards London. Hindering this action was the consideration that Hotspur's army was fresh

Wales, 1403

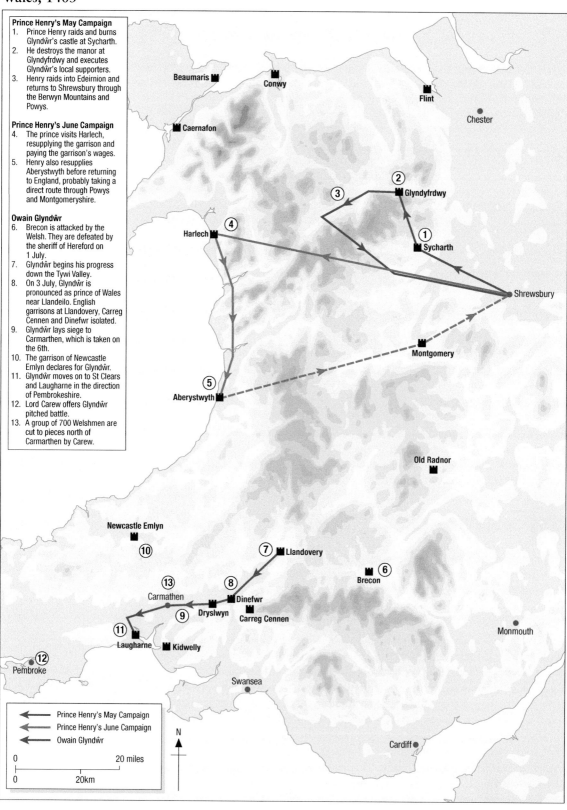

Prince Henry's May Campaign
1. Prince Henry raids and burns Glyndŵr's castle at Sycharth.
2. He destroys the manor at Glyndyfrdwy and executes Glyndŵr's local supporters.
3. Henry raids into Edeirnion and returns to Shrewsbury through the Berwyn Mountains and Powys.

Prince Henry's June Campaign
4. The prince visits Harlech, resupplying the garrison and paying the garrison's wages.
5. Henry also resupplies Aberystwyth before returning to England, probably taking a direct route through Powys and Montgomeryshire.

Owain Glyndŵr
6. Brecon is attacked by the Welsh. They are defeated by the sheriff of Hereford on 1 July.
7. Glyndŵr begins his progress down the Tywi Valley.
8. On 3 July, Glyndŵr is pronounced as prince of Wales near Llandeilo. English garrisons at Llandovery, Carreg Cennen and Dinefwr isolated.
9. Glyndŵr lays siege to Carmarthen, which is taken on the 6th.
10. The garrison of Newcastle Emlyn declares for Glyndŵr.
11. Glyndŵr moves on to St Clears and Laugharne in the direction of Pembrokeshire.
12. Lord Carew offers Glyndŵr pitched battle.
13. A group of 700 Welshmen are cut to pieces north of Carmarthen by Carew.

Beaumaris
Conwy
Flint
Chester
Caernafon
Glyndyfrdwy
Sycharth
Harlech
Shrewsbury
Montgomery
Aberystwyth
Old Radnor
Newcastle Emlyn
Llandovery
Brecon
Carmathen
Dinefwr
Dryslwyn
Carreg Cennen
Monmouth
Laugharne
Kidwelly
Pembroke
Swansea
Cardiff

Prince Henry's May Campaign
Prince Henry's June Campaign
Owain Glyndŵr

N

0   20 miles
0   20km

and still in need of further recruits. This prospect also involved leaving Prince Henry and the royal garrison for the defence of Wales untouched in its quarters in Shrewsbury. Consequently, Hotspur chose instead to march towards Shrewsbury via Whitchurch and Prees Heath. In addition to confronting Prince Henry, this move has traditionally been seen as an attempt by Hotspur to link up with the forces of Owain Glyndŵr and Edmund Mortimer. Walsingham was so certain that the two rebel leaders intended to join forces that he supposed it to be the principal reason behind the choice of Cheshire as the focal point of the rebellion. John Hardyng, in an ideal position to know his Hotspur's hopes, corroborates Walsingham's theory and says the plan was for Owain to join Hotspur near the river Severn: 'Owayn also on Seuerne hym to mete'. If this was the case, Shrewsbury was a natural choice; it had numerous strong bridges upon which armies could cross over the water, and was a natural stronghold enveloped on three sides by a bend of the river.

Despite the shared enmity of Henry IV uniting Hotspur and Glyndŵr, the extent of their collaboration is unclear. The two men had certainly been in communication in the months prior to Hotspur's arrival in Cheshire, organized through the agency of Hotspur's Denbigh esquire, William Lloyd. It is known that Lloyd travelled from Wales to Berwick in April 1403, possibly carrying messages from Glyndŵr to the Percys. Arriving on the eve of Hotspur's campaign into Scotland, it is tempting to believe that this message contained information concerning Owain's plans and may even have formed one of a series of messages designed to coordinate their campaigns.

WALES

Wales itself saw a great deal of military action during 1403. On 8 March, Prince Henry was appointed royal lieutenant in Wales, tasked with curtailing and putting down the Welsh revolt. Alongside him was a standing army of

Owain Glyndŵr's Mound at Glyndyfrdwy occupies a commanding position overlooking the Dee valley, near Corwen in Denbighshire. The manor, burned to the ground by Prince Henry in 1403, was probably located in a square moated area in the adjacent field. (Author's photograph)

four barons and bannerets, 20 knights, 500 men-at-arms, and 2,500 archers. To fulfil his commission, the prince led a raid in early May into Wales and Glyndŵr's own lordships. First, the region of Cynllaith was attacked and Glyndŵr's castle of Sycharth, elegised in a poem by Iolo Goch, burned to the ground. The English then moved on to Carrog, where a similar fate befell the park and lodge of Glyndyfrdwy, another of Glyndŵr's properties. While camping for the evening, the English conducted further raids and brought back a number of notable Welshmen as captives. In a letter dated 15 May, reporting the success of the campaign, the prince records that a particular gentleman – 'one of Owain's chieftains' – offered the sum of £500 for his life, requesting two weeks to find the money for his ransom. This plea was refused and the unfortunate man was put to death along with his companions. After these early victories the raid began to face hardship of its own. The Welsh adopted scorched earth tactics to hinder the prince's advance, causing him to order his men to carry the oats needed to feed themselves and their horses. This tactic, however, only hardened English attitudes and after Glyndyfrdwy they progressed into the county of Edeirnion in Merionethshire, ravaging the country as they went. Once this had been achieved, the English returned to Shrewsbury through the Berwyn Mountains and Powys. Although successful in its limited aim of destroying Glyndŵr's property, the raid had little effect on the course of the revolt. In the face of overwhelming force, the Welsh had simply retreated into the hills only to reappear when the English had departed. At the end of May, the prince was forced to write to his father's Council urging immediate help for the beleaguered castles of Harlech and Aberystwyth, with an urgent plea for money to pay his men. In early June an armed force was sent to relieve Harlech, soon followed by the prince himself on a flag-waving visit to both castles, bringing with him wages and supplies for the garrisons. However, such efforts did little to staunch the rising flow of Welsh discontent. The castles were isolated pockets of English control within an increasingly hostile country. The financial burden of the revolt to the English exchequer was also high. In the quarter between 17 April and 18 July, the Crown was forced to pay £5323 6s 8d, for the ongoing costs of the war, with the prince obliged to plug a shortfall amounting to £1851. These financial difficulties often meant that the soldiers went unpaid for long periods, causing the prince great difficulty in retaining them.

The English situation in Wales was made worse in early July with Glyndŵr's famous progress down the Tywi Valley in Carmarthenshire at the head of a Welsh army. For these events we are highly fortunate to be able to rely on the surviving correspondence of the English administration and loyalists in the region. In late June, a Welsh force had besieged the castle and town of Brecon. Reacting to this danger, the sheriff of Hereford, John Bodenham, marched to the town with his forces and on Sunday 1 July routed the Welsh, slaying 240 of their number. However, no sooner had the English returned home than news was received of a large uprising under Glyndŵr himself in the Tywi Valley. On Tuesday 3 July, the Welsh flocked to the rebel banner and proclaimed its leader as prince of Wales. According to English

In the poem *Llys Owain Glyndŵr* by Iolo Goch, Sycharth Castle is praised in idyllic terms: 'No want or hunger or shame, Or thirst will ever be in Sycharth.' Goch also mentions the presence of deer parks, fish ponds, rabbit-warrens, and peacocks, conjuring the image of a perfect noble retreat. Prince Henry himself called the building 'fine' before he raised it to the ground. (Author's photograph)

reports, the rebel forces numbered up to 8,240 strong. The fear of such large enemy numbers caused the English garrisons of Llandovery and Dinefwr castles to send out frantic letters appealing for help. Meanwhile, Glyndŵr spent the evening at Llandeilo, threatening the nearby castle of Carreg Cennen. The castellan, John Scudamore, was concerned enough to send a letter to the canon of Abergwili, writing that matters had deteriorated to such an extent that only a royal army under the king could hope to restore law and order. The English garrisons in the area feared that they would come under attack. However, rather than attempt to subdue these English-held castles, Glyndŵr moved on to Carmarthen, the major town of the district, laying siege for two days before the town was surrendered. As Carmarthen fell, the castle of Newcastle Emlyn, under the leadership of its Welsh castellan, Jenkin ap Llewellyn, also freely opened its gates to Glyndŵr. This was a major success and the situation for the remaining English garrisons, ensconced in their castles, looked bleak. The defending force at Dinefwr

The imposing gatehouse and castle at Harlech was a prominent symbol of English power in Wales. In 1403 the castle was visited by Prince Henry, but in the course of the Glyndŵr Rising it was captured by the Welsh. In 1405 it hosted Glyndŵr's second Welsh parliament. (Author's photograph)

even went so far as to draw up plans to abandon the castle in the dead of night and retreat back to Brecon. In the end, however, this drastic action proved unnecessary. Having achieved great success, Glyndŵr looked to keep Welsh impetus going by moving on in the direction of Pembrokeshire, having recognized the region as key to the conquest of South Wales. On 9 July they had reached St Clears, and the next day had progressed as far as Laugharne. The English power in the region was invested in Thomas, Lord Carew, who had been ordered to array troops to suppress any potential uprising. Glyndŵr sought at first to negotiate in order to allow time for him to organize and distribute the plunder from Carmarthen. Carew responded in belligerent fashion by offering pitched battle on Thursday 12 July. Wary of traditional English superiority in a formal set-piece confrontation, and fearing it could result in his capture, Glyndŵr sent a contingent of 700 men to cover his retreat. At some point north of Carmarthen, this group was waylaid by a force sent by Carew to wait in ambush and was cut to pieces. Unfortunately, it is at this point, just as the action becomes most interesting, that the letters which illuminate the Welsh campaign of 1403 abruptly come to an end. Glyndŵr's subsequent actions and the circumstances that prevented him fighting at Shrewsbury are therefore shrouded in mystery. Much depends on whether the plan was ever to meet on the Severn, as the chroniclers suggest. That this was never intended is suggested by the fact that as Hotspur was marching south from Cocklaw, Glyndŵr launched his raid into Carmarthenshire in the opposite direction to Shrewsbury. It seems, therefore, that the coordination between Hotspur and Glyndŵr, if indeed in action, was to launch simultaneous campaigns. It may even be that Glyndŵr was supposed to distract the English in South Wales and prevent them reacting to the news of the Percy rebellion.

The fall of Carmarthen to Glyndŵr was a far more significant victory than he had previously accomplished. The town and castle were surrendered to him on 6 July by the castellan, Robert Wigmore, eliciting panic from the English garrisons in the nearby area. (Author's photograph)

Unfortunately, we do not know the real reason why Glyndŵr seems to have halted his campaign into Pembrokeshire. It is possible that he did so in order to take a more active part in the Percy rebellion. This would have required a fast march back to the English border, no conclusive evidence of which survives. Instead, the chronicle sources indicate that Glyndŵr had other, more mystical concerns relating to his own safety. While in Carmarthen, Glyndŵr consulted a soothsayer – called a 'maistar of Brut' – who prophesised that he would be taken prisoner somewhere between Carmarthen and Gower, an area Glyndŵr subsequently went to great pains to avoid. The *Eulogium* also says that Glyndŵr stayed away from Shrewsbury for similar reasons, fearing treachery. The text in National Library of Wales Ms. Panton 53 suggests that Glyndŵr was in Oswestry at the date of the battle and sent a contingent of 4,000 men to Hotspur. However, this is unsupported by any other source.

If the plan was for Hotspur and Glyndŵr to join forces at Shrewsbury, the factor that neither had anticipated was the swift action of Henry IV, who arrived in Shrewsbury with his army far earlier than expected. According to Adam Usk, this was the explanation for both Glyndŵr and Northumberland's absence. Certainly, it does not appear that Hotspur, or any of the other rebels, had predicted such a fast reaction. If they had, it is unlikely that Hotspur would have faced the royal army alone.

HENRY IV

According to Walsingham, when the news of the siege of Cocklaw and the prospect of a battle with the Scots was heard, 'the whole of England's fighting men were alerted, and all the nobles of the realm and the king himself wanted to be involved in the battle'. Rather than welcoming the king's participation, however, Northumberland actively discouraged it, saying that only the lords and barons should be involved. This has raised suspicions that the Percys were using the northern campaign to recruit supporters to use against the king. Evidence for this proposition is supplied by Hardyng, who suggests that he personally witnessed letters bearing the seals of numerous lords pledged to support the Percys in the rebellion. It appears more likely, however, that Northumberland was more concerned that any victory in Scotland should be seen as the result of Percy, and not royal, action. Only then could it be claimed as the Percys' own conquest, which was in line with Henry's grant that the Percys could gain the Douglas lands only through their own military means. Given this consideration, it seems more likely that the written support seen by Hardyng was given for the campaign against the Scots, and not the subsequent rebellion.

Despite Northumberland's insistence that the Percys did not need his help, King Henry began to move north in early July. He had spent the preceding weeks in the comfortable surroundings of London, Eltham and Windsor, presumably in preparation for the campaign. Setting off from Kennington, he arrived at Newenham Priory, Bedfordshire, on 7 July and Higham Ferrers, Northamptonshire, two days later, the same day that Hotspur arrived in Chester. The next morning, he sent a letter to his council informing them of the success of Prince Henry in Wales and instructed that £1,000 be sent immediately to pay the soldiers whom his son was having difficulty retaining. Also in the letter, the king made explicit his intention of marching north to assist the earl of Northumberland and Hotspur in Scotland, after which he would go to Wales to suppress Glyndŵr's revolt in person. On this basis, historians have often believed that the king was unaware of the Percy revolt at this stage. However, the king finished the letter with an instruction informing the council to give credence to the words of its bearer, Emlyn Leget, and the esquire John Wodehouse. Sending a verbal message along with a written document was a common method of conveying secret information without the danger of setting incriminating words to paper. Under these conditions, it is impossible to know what the message contained but, given the events, it may reveal that Henry had received early rumours of the Percys' intentions. If Henry did receive an early warning, the most likely source was the earl of Dunbar. He had been involved in the Percys' Scottish campaign and the siege of Cocklaw, although appears to have been in London in early July to collect his annuity. Dunbar's intimacy with Hotspur's plans is therefore unclear, but may have involved suspicions or messages from his northern friends in a position to inform him of Hotspur's actions. Dunbar is subsequently credited for his sage advice to the king regarding Henry's choice of action. Quoting the Roman poet Lucan ('Shun, shun, delay; the ruin of the ready'), Dunbar urged Henry most forcibly not to tarry near London but to head towards the enemy and confront them. This would prevent Hotspur's forces from growing in strength while giving confidence to those who supported the king to join him in person.

The king reached Nottingham on 14 July 1403, probably spending the night in the castle. From here, he sent messages across the realm announcing his intention of moving in force against Hotspur. This image shows how the castle appeared in the late 15th century. (Author's Collection)

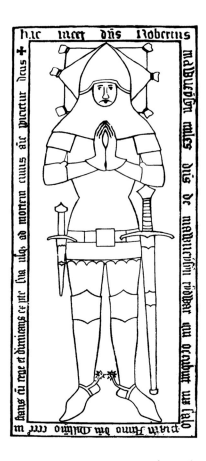

The tomb and effigy of Sir Robert Malvesyn lies in the Church of St Nicholas in Mavesyn Ridware, Staffordshire. Robert was one of many knights and men-at-arms from the surrounding counties who answered Henry IV's summons to fight. (Author's photograph)

By 12 July, the king had arrived at Leicester. Here, the rumours of the rebellion had grown and the king sent a letter to his council ordering them to stop anybody leaving the country without the king's permission, to prevent ill-words from reaching his enemies. On the 14th the king was in Nottingham. By now the king must have received firm news of Hotspur's proclamations in Chester. He responded by sending messages across the kingdom appealing for support and announcing his intention of marching against the rebels in force. One such letter, sent to Coventry, includes details of the king's situation and awareness of Hotspur's position. It is evident that Henry had received detailed reports of Hotspur's movements through Cheshire, which led him to believe that the rebels' intention was to march into Wales and link up with Glyndŵr. Fear of this prospect is possibly what spurred Henry into action, anxious that the strength of his enemies should not combine. Henry also makes clear that he had received several letters of support from Cheshire and Northumberland. This is interesting as it may provide a glimpse of evidence that Henry was also being kept informed of Northumberland's progress in the north.

From Nottingham the king turned west towards Shrewsbury, marching past Derby and arriving in Burton upon Trent on the 16th. Prior to his arrival in the town there is little evidence that the king made considerable efforts to recruit large numbers of armed men, perhaps because he was still uncertain of the full scale and danger of the Percy revolt. Other sources suggest the king had, instead, made serious attempts to end the revolt through mediation. The *Dieulacres Chronicle* says that on the 16th the king wrote 'a friendly letter' to Hotspur 'naming him his beloved kinsman and warmly asked him to come to him or let him know what he purposed by a trustworthy envoy, and to make sufficient amends as far as was in his power'. The envoy who carried the letter returned to the king without a reply. At the same time a second letter was sent to Hotspur's father. Walsingham records that when the king received news that the earl was still in the north, he quickly imagined that Hotspur alone was the instigator of the rebellion, driven by the 'obstinate malice of [his] youth'. He then 'determined at once to meet Percy … before they could gather an army to attack'.

From Burton Henry sent an order to the sheriffs of the nearby counties to collect all knights, esquires and valets as speedily as possible. At the same time, less welcome reports reached him concerning the uncertain loyalties of some of his subjects. On 16 July, Henry issued a mandate to Sir John Pudesay, Sir Robert de Hilton, Sir Gerard Salveyn and ten others to attend him within six days. Evidently, however, Henry changed his mind and on the very same day issued another mandate addressed to the sheriff of York, ordering him to take the men into custody. On 18 July, he issued a similar order for Thomas, Lord de la Warre to present himself at once, on pain of forfeiting life and limb.

The campaign required money and, on the 17th, Henry sent a message to his council ordering all to hasten to him, apart from the treasurer who was to remain behind for the purpose of raising loans. The records show Henry had already been active in acquiring funds, having borrowed £1,000

The march to Shrewsbury

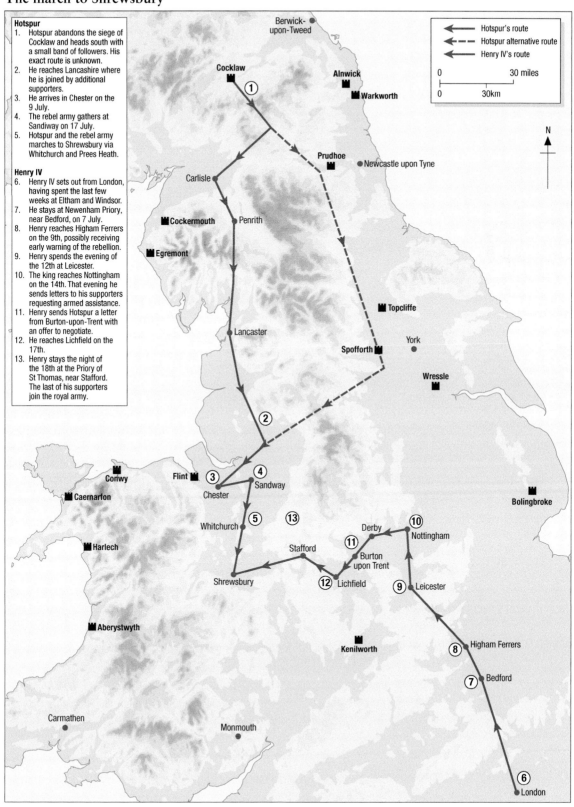

Hotspur
1. Hotspur abandons the siege of Cocklaw and heads south with a small band of followers. His exact route is unknown.
2. He reaches Lancashire where he is joined by additional supporters.
3. He arrives in Chester on the 9 July.
4. The rebel army gathers at Sandiway on 17 July.
5. Hotspur and the rebel army marches to Shrewsbury via Whitchurch and Prees Heath.

Henry IV
6. Henry IV sets out from London, having spent the last few weeks at Eltham and Windsor.
7. He stays at Newenham Priory, near Bedford, on 7 July.
8. Henry reaches Higham Ferrers on the 9th, possibly receiving early warning of the rebellion.
9. Henry spends the evening of the 12th at Leicester.
10. The king reaches Nottingham on the 14th. That evening he sends letters to his supporters requesting armed assistance.
11. Henry sends Hotspur a letter from Burton-upon-Trent with an offer to negotiate.
12. He reaches Lichfield on the 17th.
13. Henry stays the night of the 18th at the Priory of St Thomas, near Stafford. The last of his supporters join the royal army.

Hotspur's route
Hotspur alternative route
Henry IV's route

0   30 miles
0   30km

N

Berwick-upon-Tweed
Cocklaw
Alnwick
Warkworth
Prudhoe
Newcastle upon Tyne
Carlisle
Cockermouth
Penrith
Egremont
Topcliffe
Lancaster
Spofforth
York
Wressle
Conwy
Flint
Sandway
Caernarfon
Chester
Bolingbroke
Whitchurch
Derby
Nottingham
Harlech
Stafford
Burton upon Trent
Shrewsbury
Lichfield
Leicester
Aberystwyth
Kenilworth
Higham Ferrers
Bedford
Carmathen
Monmouth
London

45

Hotspur's demands that his army be allowed to enter Shrewsbury were forcibly refused by the town's authorities. His army was preparing to lay siege when Henry IV unexpectedly arrived in the area. (British Library, Ms. Royal 20 C VII, f. 29)

from a group of London merchants. On the 16th, £666 was delivered to the king in Burton and the same amount sent to the prince in Shrewsbury. Oddly, £666 was also sent to Northumberland and Hotspur for the wages of their northern retainers although, presumably, this had been sent a few days previously while the king was still unaware of the revolt. On the way to the battle Henry also managed to borrow 2,500 marks from Lewys de Portico, a merchant of Lucca.

On the evening of the 17th Henry reached Lichfield, from where he sent a letter to Edmund Stafford, earl of Stafford, and Robert Fraunceys, sheriff of Stafford, with a request to gather all the armed men they could muster. This was followed on the 18th by Henry's final call for men, this time to all the knights, squires and others in his pay in the Welsh marches. That evening the king lodged in the Priory of St Thomas, near Stafford, a location chosen to allow the last of his supporters to reach him. All present in the army must have anticipated an imminent battle. In this tense atmosphere Henry still had an eye on the rest of his kingdom. In order to prevent unrest, he wrote to the sheriffs of London, Essex, Hertfordshire and Middlesex, instructing them to prohibit publication of any 'sinister news' from the marches of Wales. After these final actions had been completed, the royal army began the final 30-mile march to Shrewsbury. Passing the Roman town of Viroconium (Wroxeter) they crossed the river Severn at Attingham Bridge (now Atcham) and arrived outside the walls of Shrewsbury on Friday 20 July.

While the king had been making his progress towards the Welsh marches, Hotspur had not been idle and had marched his men from Sandiway to Shrewsbury. In addition to the many strategic advantages to be gained by taking the town, another crucial factor in Hotspur's mind was the presence of his uncle, Thomas Percy, earl of Worcester, in the garrison at Shrewsbury. Thomas had been serving as the prince's guardian and governor and was the effective second-in-command of the English forces on the border. At some

Shrewsbury Castle was the headquarters of the English garrison during Prince Henry's Welsh campaigns in 1403. When the earl of Worcester absconded to the rebel side he took a large contingent of the garrison with him. Today, the castle is home to the Shropshire Regimental Museum. (Author's photograph)

point before the 20th, however, Worcester slipped away from the town and defected to his nephew. Frustratingly little is known about this event but it seems likely that this action had been planned for some time. Walsingham suggests that Worcester brought with him money and treasures stolen from the prince's house in London to pay Hotspur's troops. When he left, the earl managed to persuade a significant proportion of the garrison to join him in the rebellion. Worcester had indentured to supply 40 men-at-arms and 200 archers to the Welsh campaigns, the largest contingent outside of the prince's own. However, when he departed Shrewsbury, Worcester managed to take with him five knights, 96 esquires and 866 archers. It may have been Worcester's original intention to take the prince captive. If so, the large number who remained loyal to the young Henry – perhaps as many as 1,200 – prevented this from becoming a practical option.

The friar and historian John Capgrave tells us that the rebel army was the first to reach Shrewsbury, probably on 19 July, upon which they immediately began to lay siege to the town. Some fighting took place and some of the outlying suburbs were burned. The burgesses later claimed that this was done to save the town, and possibly included the removal of buildings abutting the walls to prevent enemy scaling. However, what the rebels did not expect was the imminent arrival of the king the following day. Walsingham records that Hotspur had thought Henry was still awaiting his council in Burton upon Trent, some 50 miles distant. The sight of the king's banners forced the rebel army to quit their siegeworks and retire to the north-west, encamping for the evening near the hamlet of Berwick. To Walsingham, the name of the settlement was providential as it shared the same name as the famous border fortress of Berwick-upon-Tweed. According to an apocryphal folk-tale of the battle, the next day Hotspur found that he had left his favourite sword behind. When he asked where it was, he was told 'it was at a small farmstead in his rear called Berwick'. Upon hearing this he turned pale, to the surprise of the by-standers, and said with a deep sigh to his servant: 'My plough I see is reaching the end of the furrow, for it was told me by a seer, when I was yet in my own country, that I should verily die at Berwick. But; woe to me! the double meaning of the name has beguiled me.' The same evening was spent by the royal army crossing the Severn near Uffington, before they bivouacked for the night in the fields surrounding Haughmond Abbey.

The Augustinian Haughmond Abbey was founded in the 12th century, a few miles east of Shrewsbury. On 20 July 1403, the surrounding fields hosted the royal army on the eve of the battle. Henry IV probably spent the evening more comfortably within the abbey's walls. (Author's photograph)

THE BATTLE

With both of the armies north of the river Severn, separated by only five miles of open countryside, the stage was set for the coming battle. The continued proximity of the royal army prevented any hope of the rebels retreating or escaping. This measure would have inevitably led to the piecemeal disintegration and destruction of the rebel army through desertion and enemy harassment. Even at this late stage, Hotspur and Worcester may still have hoped for reinforcements under Northumberland or Glyndŵr. However, both must have been aware that their main hope of success lay in their ability to secure favourable ground for the upcoming battle.

THE BATTLEFIELD

The battle of Shrewsbury is traditionally said to have taken place north of the city, in the fields surrounding the village subsequently named Battlefield. Nevertheless, the exact location of the battle has been of some debate among historians. The name of the field in which the battle took place is variously given by the sources as Old Field, Bull Field, Hatelyfield, Hussey Field, Berwick Field and Hynsifeld. This confusion may be partially explained by the fact that medieval armies took up a considerable amount of space as they moved across the landscape. Additionally, the fighting area almost certainly

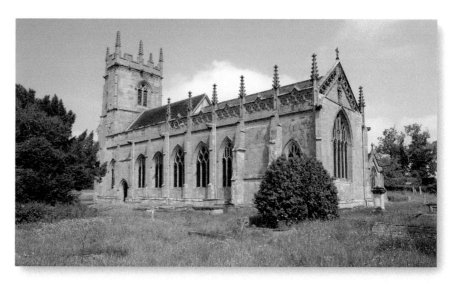

Battlefield Church was begun in 1406 and dedicated to St Mary Magdalene as a college of secular priests. Built for the salvation of the king's soul and for those killed during the battle, it was traditionally thought to be built on the site of a mass grave. (Author's photograph)

The Shrewsbury battlefield

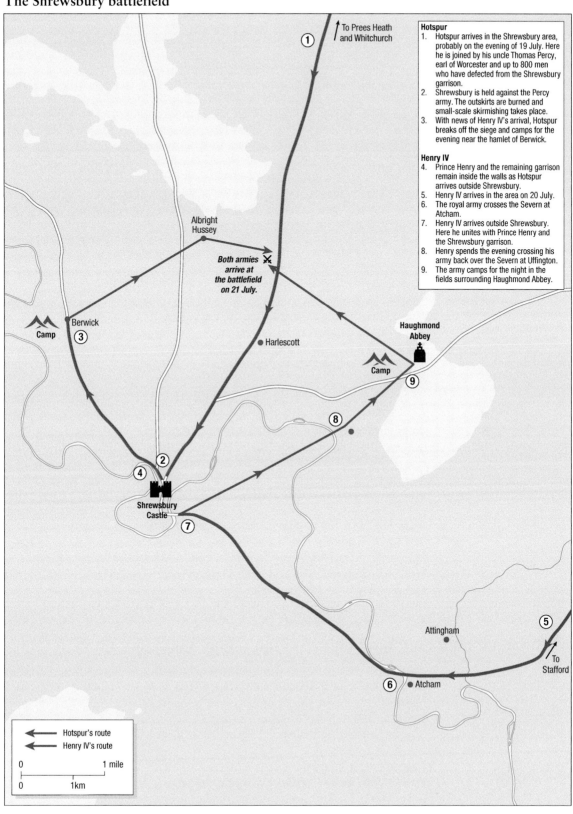

To Prees Heath and Whitchurch

Hotspur
1. Hotspur arrives in the Shrewsbury area, probably on the evening of 19 July. Here he is joined by his uncle Thomas Percy, earl of Worcester and up to 800 men who have defected from the Shrewsbury garrison.
2. Shrewsbury is held against the Percy army. The outskirts are burned and small-scale skirmishing takes place.
3. With news of Henry IV's arrival, Hotspur breaks off the siege and camps for the evening near the hamlet of Berwick.

Henry IV
4. Prince Henry and the remaining garrison remain inside the walls as Hotspur arrives outside Shrewsbury.
5. Henry IV arrives in the area on 20 July.
6. The royal army crosses the Severn at Atcham.
7. Henry IV arrives outside Shrewsbury. Here he unites with Prince Henry and the Shrewsbury garrison.
8. Henry spends the evening crossing his army back over the Severn at Uffington.
9. The army camps for the night in the fields surrounding Haughmond Abbey.

Albright Hussey

Both armies arrive at the battlefield on 21 July.

Berwick

Camp

Harlescott

Haughmond Abbey

Camp

Shrewsbury Castle

Attingham

To Stafford

Atcham

Hotspur's route
Henry IV's route

0   1 mile
0   1km

A panorama of the battlefield showing the character of the terrain. In 1403, the landscape was devoid of many of the post-medieval structures now in evidence and was managed through the open field system of agriculture commonly in use during the Middle Ages. Battlefield Church can be seen in the far distance. (Author's photograph)

encompassed more than a single field. This was especially true once the battle had been decided and the combatants splintered into groups, some fleeing the scene while others went after them in pursuit.

The written sources offer little that can help us locate the battlefield with more precision. Our best source, the *Dieulacres Chronicle*, says that the battle took place in the fields near Harlescott, north of Shrewsbury. Jean de Waurin, whose description of the site of the battlefield is customarily short, notes only that the rebel army chose the most defensible ground. Walsingham was more principally concerned with the nature of the terrain. He provides us with the detail that Hotspur used the local vegetation to his advantage. The battlefield was thickly sown with peas and so Hotspur directed his men to loop and twine the tendrils of the plants together in order to hamper the advance of the royal army.

One source that does provide more information of the battlefield location is Adam Usk. He says that the battle took place two miles from Shrewsbury in a field later used by Henry IV to found an establishment for the souls of those slain during the battle. This foundation, begun in 1406, was dedicated to St Mary Magdalene but is more popularly known today as Battlefield Church. The founding charter of the building makes it clear that it was built in the same field in which the battle took place. This document would seemingly locate the battle with some precision. Some uncertainties, however, complicate the issue. After the battle, the number of bodies would have prevented all but the most important individuals from being transported any great distance for burial. Several sources mention the existence of a mass grave that was dug nearby for the corpses. Popular belief has long held that the church was built above, or nearby, the site of the pit. Finding the mass grave would therefore allow us to precisely define the location of the battlefield. In 1903, Reverend W. G. D. Fletcher wrote that 'many years ago' workmen installing a drain in the north of the chancel cut through large masses of human bones. In the 1860s more unidentified bodies, this time in lead coffins, were found under the floor of the church during repairs. Recent archaeological excavation in the churchyard, however, found no trace of the these burials in the precincts of the church, and so the location of the mass grave remains unresolved.

Some modern historians have attempted to move the battlefield from its traditional location. Local priest Father Stephen Maxfield, re-investigating documents and chronicles published after the anniversary of the battle in 2003, has placed the battlefield further to the west, between Broad Oak and Harlescott. Against this interpretation, however, stands the archaeological record. The English naturalist Charles Darwin, who was born and lived in Shrewsbury during the early 19th century, recorded that a large number of arrowheads were unearthed in a field north of Shrewsbury during ploughing. Unfortunately, Darwin failed to give precise details of the field in question. Despite this, however, his description fits well with the traditional location of the battle. Luckily, more recent evidence also supports the traditional area around Battlefield Church. During work carried out alongside the TV series *Two Men in a Trench*, the fields north of Battlefield Church were found to contain numerous finds congruous with those expected of a medieval battlefield. These included numerous bodkin arrowheads, a sword tip and scabbard chape and possibly the tip of a war-hammer. A larger number of small iron finds, too corroded to identify precisely, were also recorded.

The excavated field forms part of a raised ridge running east from the Whitchurch road to Albright Hussey, rising immediately to the north of Battlefield Church. This ground would have provided some of the only favourable terrain available to Hotspur in the area. The ridge was also bordered by major roads in existence during the 15th century, allowing large numbers of armed men to reach and access the field easily. For these reasons, there is no reason to doubt the traditional placement of the battlefield, as it perfectly fits with the known historical and archaeological facts.

FORMATION AND NEGOTIATIONS

Hotspur and the rebel army were the first to arrive at the battlefield. Given their numerical inferiority and the considerable shock of Henry's arrival, the advantage of choosing the ground on which to fight must have been an important consideration. Keeping morale high was also critical, especially during the period when Henry IV and the royalist army reached the field and drew up in sight of the rebels. As daunting to the rebels as their enemies' superior numbers must have been the array of standards, each belonging to a great member of the nobility, unfurled among the royal army. Central, and most important, among these would have been the personal device of Henry IV and the royal banner featuring the arms of England. It was possibly at this point that the reality of the rebellion dawned upon the more naïve members of Hotspur's army. On 30 July, Henry IV issued a pardon to Richard Horkesley for his unusual part in the battle. Although Horkesley had initially joined the rebel cause, once he saw the royal banner he changed his mind and forsook Hotspur, crossing over to fight for the king. The pardon gives no indication of the exact timing of this defection. It is probable that Horkesley abandoned Hotspur when the king first arrived at Shrewsbury, but it is also possible that he switched sides on the battlefield itself during the opening negotiations. The episode demonstrates the potency of the royal image and the psychological difficulty faced by contemporary Englishmen in raising arms against the anointed king.

The wearing of livery badges was a prominent means of displaying affiliation with a particular lord or family. Badges were, therefore, often given out by the nobility to men in their service. From left to right: the Stafford knot; Henry IV's 'SOVEREYGNE' feather; Richard II's white hart; the Percy crescent. (Author's collection)

The formation that both armies adopted at Shrewsbury is one of the hardest features of the battle to reconstruct. The most common formation adopted by medieval commanders was to divide their armies into three distinct units: the vanguard; main body and rearguard. These divisions would be most commonly be set out in a line, with the rearguard on the left, the main body in the centre and the vanguard on the right. Jean de Waurin suggests that the royal army was divided in just this way, with the king taking the central command in the middle of his army. However, the two earliest and most reliable sources do not explicitly support this idea. The *Dieulacres Chronicle* says that the royal army was drawn up in three lines: the earl of Stafford led the king's first line (*'Comes ergo Staffordie qui primam aciem'*); the king was placed in the second line (*'rex in secunda acie'*) and Prince Henry was in the third (*'princeps Henricus cum tercia acie'*). To decipher what this meant, we are dependent on the translation of the Latin word *acies*, which was often the term given to a specific division of the battle. If taken in this context it could, therefore, be plausibly argued that what is meant is that the royal army deployed in a highly standard medieval formation – in three divisions, one under the king's personal command and the others under Prince Henry and the earl of Stafford. One difficulty with this interpretation, however, is that *acies* can also be used to refer to a specific rank within a single division. Walsingham clearly describes Stafford as being entrusted with 'the front rank (*anterior acies*) of the king's division'. This suggests that Stafford was in the front line of the main central body of the army commanded by the king. However, Walsingham's account of the royal formation only mentions two divisions, one commanded by the king and the other by the prince, and neglects to give information as to the existence or position of a third. This formation and division of command would be highly unusual, although not entirely unprecedented, among armies of the period. On balance, therefore, it seems likely that Henry IV deployed in a standard formation of three divisions in a line with Prince Henry on the left and the king himself in the centre, with Stafford the most likely commander of the right. This interpretation makes most sense of the text of the *Dieulacres Chronicle* and concurs with later sources such as Raphael Holinshed and John Hayward, both of whom are firm in their placement of the earl of Stafford in the royal 'foreward'. Another plausible interpretation of the sources is that the royal army advanced in echelon, with the right wing slightly ahead of the other two divisions.

Hotspur's formation is equally problematic and is almost entirely neglected in the early sources. Edward Hall describes the 'Scottes', probably commanded by the earl of Douglas, taking the 'forward' of Hotspur's army. From his description of events, it seems likely that Hall meant that Douglas was arrayed on the left of the rebel army, directly opposite the royal right wing. This interpretation was followed by followed by the 16th-century English chroniclers Holinshed and Hayward who describe the combat on this side of the battle in detail. However, as with Stafford in the royal army, locating the earl of Douglas' position within the rebel formation presents significant difficulties. From the description of his actions during the battle, it is hard to understand how he can have begun the battle so far from

The seal of Thomas Percy features a prominent display of Percy heraldry and identifies him as the earl of Worcester. According to several sources, Thomas was the main reason behind the failure of the negotiations between Henry IV and Hotspur. (Society of Antiquaries)

Hotspur's own position. Given Douglas' recent status as a prisoner of the Percys, it is also difficult to believe that Hotspur would have presented the earl with such a crucial role well out of his own sight and control. Hotspur himself appears to have taken command of the rebel centre, the most prominent position, opposite and directly opposed to the king. Worcester's role and actions during the battle are entirely unknown. It is likely, however, given his rank that he took command of one of the three divisions, probably the Percy vanguard opposite Prince Henry. This interpretation of the royal and rebel deployment is dependent on traditional modes of thinking about the constitution and leadership of a medieval army. However, if the armies were smaller than traditionally estimated, it is possible that less formal and regimented formations were used.

View down from the position taken up by the rearguard of the rebel army. Modern industrial buildings and a railway line now impede the view towards Shrewsbury. (Author's photograph)

At the battles of Crécy in 1346, Poitiers in 1356 and, later, at Agincourt in 1415, the archers serving in the English army appear to have formed up in greatest numbers on the flanks, either side of the body of men-at-arms. If this was a normal tactic deployed by English armies, it appears from the scant available evidence that it was consciously disregarded at Shrewsbury. This might be a further sign that both armies were substantially smaller than other English armies deployed during the period. Walsingham records that before marshalling his own men, Henry IV first surveyed the enemy army 'drawn up against him with the archers in front'. From this we can imagine that the divisions of Hotspur's army were each fronted by archers. At Crécy, Froissart describes the archers as being organized *en herce*, or a harrow formation. This is occasionally interpreted as meaning that they were formed up in a series of triangular wedges. At other times archers are described as forming up in a chequered fashion. With such a lack of evidence, we cannot be certain what, if any, form the archers at Shrewsbury took at the beginning of the battle. In whichever formation they initially took to the field, it is likely that once the arrows began to fall any prior organization soon descended into a more loose and chaotic form.

With the armies within sight but not bowshot of each other, several hours of negotiations took place, initiated by the king and involving numerous envoys passing backwards and forwards between the two positions. To begin the talks, the abbots of Shrewsbury and Haughmond, with the Clerk of the Privy Seal, were sent by the king to the rebels to discuss their grievances and explore the possibility of a peaceful solution. The accounts of the resulting talks vary extensively, although most agree that Henry IV was conciliatory, taking the initiative to avoid bloodshed. According to Walsingham, Hotspur was placated by the emollient nature of the king's initial overtures and sent his uncle Worcester as an envoy to talk with the king privately and negotiate a redress to their grievances. The king indicated that he was prepared to discuss the entire matter and sent Worcester back to relay this to Hotspur. However, when the earl returned he 'thwarted the business by reporting the opposite of the king's replies', embittering Hotspur and making battle inevitable. The account continues that while waiting for a reply, the earl of Dunbar advised the king against negotiations, arguing that they were simply a means devised by the rebels to buy time for the arrival of reinforcements.

The *Dieulacres Chronicle* agrees with Walsingham as to the importance of Worcester as an envoy. However, there is no mention of the earl lying to Hotspur about the king's words. When the king asked the reason for the revolt, the earl straightaway replied that 'the cause was the unjust seizure of the crown which by the law of inheritance should go to the son of the earl of March. Thereupon the king proposed to depart without slaughter and to go to parliament, notwithstanding the fact that he had been elected by them and the lords.' Another of the allegations levelled at the king was that he had sworn to Hotspur and his father on the relics of Bridlington that he would never aim for the crown, claiming the duchy of Lancaster was enough for him, and that if anyone worthier of the crown were to be found, he would willingly yield to him. In response to these provocations we are told that Henry offered to fight a duel with Hotspur to avoid further bloodshed. This proposal, as well as the offer to submit the quarrel to parliament, was rejected.

The accounts of Walsingham and Dieulacres Abbey are deeply favourable towards King Henry and at pains to excuse him from any charge of responsibility for the battle. Another account offering an alternative interpretation is that of John Hardyng, closely reproduced by Edward Hall. According to this account, the king was sent the Percy manifesto 'in the field' by Hotspur's esquires, Thomas Knayton and Roger Salvayn. The charges were damning and accused Henry of lying to the Percys in his intentions towards the crown, ignoring the rival claims of the earl of March, raising excessive taxes, surrounding himself with evil councillors, overriding the law, packing parliament with supporters and failing to ransom Edmund Mortimer, among other crimes. The most serious accusation, however, was the charge that Henry had usurped the crown and murdered Richard II. This ran:

> Also we do allege, saie & entende to prove, that were thou sworest to us upon the same Gospelles in theforsaied place and tyme, that our soueraigne lorde and thyne, kyng Richarde, should reigne duryng the terme of his life in his royall prerogative and dignitee: thou hast caused the same our soveraigne lorde and thine, traitorously within the castell of Poumfret [Pontefract], without the consent or lodgement of the lordes of the realme, by the space of fiftene daies and so many nightes whiche is horible among Christian people to be heard with honger, thirst and colde to perishe, to be murdered. Wherefore thou art perjured and false.

The last sentence was repeated numerous times throughout the document at the end of each charge. After the direct accusation of unlawful usurpation and murder was made there was little chance of compromise. The lawful nature of the usurpation, with the assent of lords and commons, was the basis of Henry's claim to legitimacy and so he could not concede such a point – or allow the matter to go to arbitration – without compromising his dignity. In addition, it is very unlikely that either side had realistic hopes of a peaceful outcome. Henry was not in a position to submit to the rebel manifesto without a fight, while Hotspur and Worcester's army had largely been recruited on the promise of overthrowing the king. Moreover, the rising had gone too far for either side to back down. If the king wished to keep his throne and prevent future uprisings, he could not allow such behaviour to go unpunished. To the Percys, only Henry's removal now offered the chance to guarantee their future prospects.

This manuscript image from the late 14th century depicting the battle of Courtrai (1302) vividly illustrates the carnage of mêlée combat. A variety of hand weapons such as swords, hammers, daggers and poleaxes can be seen in use, while the bodies of the injured and the dead pile up below the feet of the combatants. (British Library, Ms. Royal 20 C VII, f. 34)

At the final stage of the negotiations, some sources claim that Henry became angry and made accusations of his own against Hotspur, alleging to know the true reason behind the revolt. According to the *Dieulacres Chronicle*, Henry exclaimed: 'I confess that your wicked plan has been divulged which, as long as I live, will never happen. Your purpose is to … crown as King Henry Percy or his son by reason of his wife's right to inheritance.'

According to Capgrave, who provides an unlikely transcript of the conversation between Worcester and the king, Henry then exculpated himself from blame for all that was to come, and prayed 'that thou [meaning Worcester and Hotspur] must answer for all the blood that here shall be shed this day and not I'.

THE BATTLE BEGINS

Once the negotiations had broken down, there was no option but to fight it out. According to the *Dieulacres Chronicle*, the day was drawing down to the hour of vespers, the canonical time for evening prayers that began near sunset. The opposing armies had been waiting in full sight of each other for most of the day. According to Walsingham, this had so riled the men that 'the signal [for battle] was needless, so eager were both sides for the fray'. It is unlikely that many of the men assembled could have appreciated the true nature of the fight to come. The exceptional brutality of the battle is agreed by all the sources. The *Dieulacres Chronicle* reported that 'never in the whole world was such a great host thought to have been destroyed in battle in the space of two hours'. This was all the more shocking as those being killed were almost entirely fellow Englishmen.

The view from Prince Henry's initial position on the battlefield, looking up the slope on which Hotspur had formed the rebel army. Modern houses on the right of the picture have disrupted the view towards Battlefield Farm. (Author's photograph)

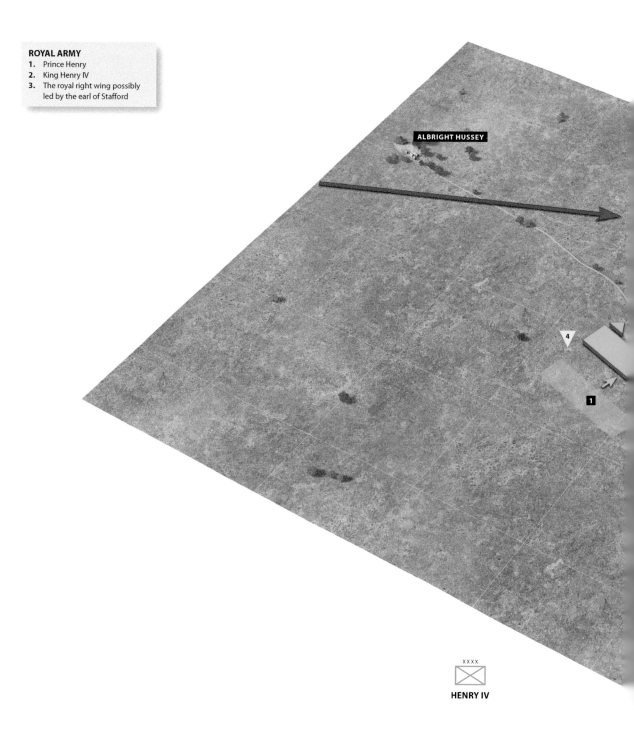

ROYAL ARMY
1. Prince Henry
2. King Henry IV
3. The royal right wing possibly led by the earl of Stafford

ALBRIGHT HUSSEY

4

1

XXXX
HENRY IV

EVENTS

1. Hotspur and the rebel army arrive at the battlefield first and take up position on the high ground to the east of Albright Hussey.

2. Henry IV arrives later and forms up to the south of the site of Battlefield Church.

3. Negotiations between the two sides take most of the day. By the time talks break down it is early evening.

4. With both sides eager to fight, the armies begin to move towards each other.

5. The archers in Hotspur's army are drawn up in front of the infantry, a formation likely copied by Henry IV. Once in range, as close as 100–150 yards, the Cheshire archers in Hotspur's army begin the battle by firing upon the royal lines.

Note: Gridlines are shown at intervals of 250m

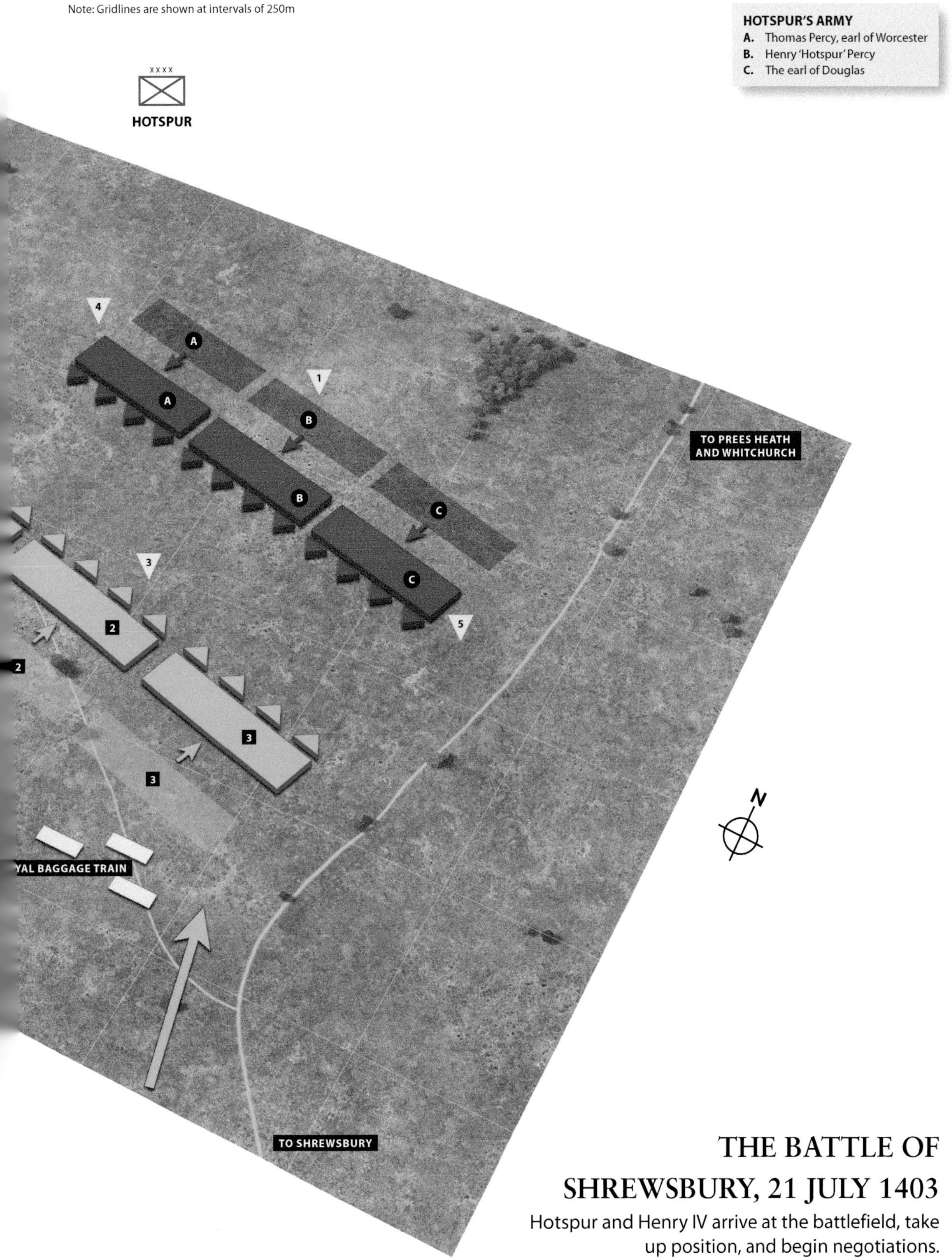

xxxx

HOTSPUR

4

A

A

1

B

B

C

C

3

2

2

5

3

3

TO PREES HEATH AND WHITCHURCH

N

YAL BAGGAGE TRAIN

TO SHREWSBURY

THE BATTLE OF
SHREWSBURY, 21 JULY 1403
Hotspur and Henry IV arrive at the battlefield, take up position, and begin negotiations.

As with so many other medieval battles, there is little agreement in the sources about the sequence of events or the involvement of named individuals in key moments. The opening move of the battle seems to have been a general advance by the king and the royal army onto the ridge on which the rebel army was positioned. This forward move would have been accompanied by a great clamour and noise. According to Hayward, this included 'the notes of furie, the soundes of slaughter, the harmonie of hell: trumpettes, fifes, drumms, musicke sutable to the mirth at hand', and was designed to encourage and raise the spirits of the men. It was in the king's interest to force the battle before the approaching darkness of night made it impossible. This was particularly important as the next day was Sunday, the holy day upon which fighting was strictly prohibited by the Church. Henry feared that this delay could provide the time needed for reinforcements to join the rebels. Hotspur's inferior numbers provided him with ample reason to remain in place with his army on the ridge, from where his archers could take advantage of the higher ground to shoot arrows down on the approaching foe. The king's advance, however, may have provoked a smaller but similar move forward by Hotspur in order to keep morale high among his men.

As soon as the royal army was in a good range the Cheshire archers opened the attack. Accurately calculating the shooting rate for medieval archers is notoriously difficult, although a rate of ten per minute should have been within the upper capability of every trained man. All equipped archers would have been expected to carry two full sheaves with them, totalling around 48 arrows, which could have been resupplied as the battle progressed. The percentage of archers in the respective armies is unknown. However, it was characteristic of the period that the army consisted of more archers than men-at-arms. A conservative estimate would therefore put several thousand archers in each army, perhaps around the 4,000–5,000 mark. A figure of 40,000–50,000 arrows per minute from each army is therefore a plausible number and lends truth to the fabled image of the 'arrow storm'. Although such a sustained rate of fire may have dropped as individuals tired or were killed, the number of arrows in the air at the opening of the battle must have truly staggered and horrified those present. Waurin says that the archers drew so fast and thick that it seemed to the onlookers like a thick cloud. Walsingham records how fatally destructive this cloud was to the royal side as the arrows fell: 'The place for arrows was not in the ground … for men fell on the king's side as fast as leaves fall in autumn after the hoar-frost. Nor did the king's archers fail to do their work, but sent a shower of sharp-points against their adversaries.'

This was the first battle in which the fabled English longbow had been used on both sides in such large numbers. During Henry V's later campaigns and the Wars of the Roses, this form of warfare became expected and tactics developed accordingly. At Shrewsbury neither side had the opportunity to anticipate or prepare. The protection one could have against this form of warfare depended very much on the status of the individual and his personal wealth. The best-quality armour of the period provided excellent protection against all but the most stubborn or freak arrow. The higher classes and noblemen wore full-plate armour covering almost the entirety of their bodies. Less wealthy and lower-rank individuals would have significantly less protection, and wore leather and hardened cloth jerkins, mail and more partial plate armours. Against such defences the arrows could have a deadly effect. The impact of an arrow was capable of shattering bone or penetrating deep into the flesh, incapacitating the victim or killing him outright. The scene at Shrewsbury must therefore have been terrible, with men falling wounded or dead in great numbers, many with terrible wounds to their heads, bodies and limbs. Even the men-at-arms, protected against the worst of the arrows in their full armours, would have been hit, perhaps multiple times, with the impact of the arrows enough to bruise, wind and panic the wearer. Against this onslaught men could not be trained. Even if an individual escaped being wounded himself, the psychological impact of seeing compatriots fall, combined with the terrible fear of being hit next, must have been truly severe.

No source tells us how long the arrow storm lasted, but considering the number of arrows it cannot have been much longer than five minutes. Although the destruction and casualties on both sides must have been heavy, it appears that the superior skill, higher ground and the obstacle of the entangled peas had combined to give the rebels the best of the exchange. At some point, probably soon after the first arrows had found their targets, a significant proportion of the royal right wing broke and fled. Walsingham records that as many as 4,000 turned in flight, thinking that the king could not have survived. The *Dieulacres Chronicle* adds that as they quit the field, they raided the royal baggage, taking their fellows' carts and horses. The truth of this story is indicated by the pardon granted to one Henry Parker after the battle 'for having lately taken and carried away one pair of our [Henry IV's] daggers, or knives, and seven of our spoons of gold and silver, in our battle near Salop'. Additionally, the records show that many were recompensed for the loss of horses, armour and other goods, much of which was probably stolen while their owners were involved in the fighting. For example, Richard de Croke was pardoned and cleared of his debt amounting to the large sum of £26 6s 8d, as he and his sons were 'with the archers, and his two sons were wounded, and he lost his horses and harness'.

It may have been at this point in the battle – although the sources are contradictory – that the earl of Stafford was killed. The *Dieulacres Chronicle* says that he died along with his men after being hit by an arrow. If Stafford was in command of the right wing, his death would likely have precipitated the rout, as described. It is also possible that Stafford died near the king in the front line of the central battle. Later sources such as Holinshed and Hayward, however, suggest otherwise and say that the men-at-arms on the eastern side of the battle under Stafford and Douglas clashed in hand-to-hand combat. According to the latter, the royal soldiers advanced in a loose formation but met with a more organized and determined enemy who caused them to break, with Stafford being struck down as his men retreated. Hayward is

THE BATTLE BEGINS AS HOTSPUR'S CHESHIRE ARCHERS LOOSE THEIR ARROWS AT THE ROYAL ARMY (PP. 60–61)

Although his account of the battle of Shrewsbury is a mixture of fact and fiction, Jean de Waurin in his *Recueil des croniques et anchiennes istories de la Grant Bretaigne* provides a vivid description of the arrow storm unleashed by both sides: 'The archers dismounted uttering a loud and terrible cry which was terrible to hear, and then began to march at a good pace and in good order against each other, and the archers drew so fast and thick that it seemed to the beholders like a thick cloud, for the sun which at that time was bright and clear then lost its brightness so thick were the arrows.'

In this picture Hotspur **(1)** can be seen in discussions with Sir Richard Venables and Sir Richard Vernon, two of the Cheshire knights mentioned in the sources. His armour is decorated with bands of gilded metal, a great expense marking him out as an important and wealthy individual on the battlefield. Behind him, his standard-bearer holds Hotspur's arms of the Percy lion quartered with the three pikes (*Esox lucius*) of the de Lucy family

(2). His arms also feature a label of three points, indicative of his status as the eldest son of his father Henry Percy, earl of Northumberland. In front of Hotspur, the Cheshire and Welsh archers **(3)** have begun to shoot at their foes in the royal army. Some wear the livery of Percy, with crescent badges acting as a symbol of their allegiance. Others wear the white and green livery associated with Richard II. The *English Chronicle* says that Hotspur himself donned a green and white tunic at Sandiway in order to show his commitment to the rebel cause. In addition to their longbows, the archers carry an assortment of weapons including swords and rondel daggers **(4)**, designed for close-quarters combat and to dispatch men-at-arms by stabbing them through the gaps in their armour. In the distance the royal army can be seen, having already suffered numerous casualties. On the left of the picture **(5)**, the royal vanguard can be seen beginning to turn and break in response to the ferocity of the rebel's arrow storm.

alone in this description of the battle, however, and Holinshed's account makes it clear that Stafford was able to extricate himself and join Henry IV in the main body of the army.

With the royal vanguard partially disintegrated and the general royal advance halted by the arrow onslaught, the initiative of the battle now lay with Hotspur. The disarray among the royal army must have presented a tempting target for attack. The loss of the royal right also meant that the discrepancy in numbers between the armies had been reduced, giving the rebels their best chance of success if they could press their early momentum. Additionally, now that battle had well and truly been joined, the Percys had only one available option – to isolate and kill the king in the field. Accordingly, Hotspur launched an attack down the slope of the ridge. With cries of 'Esperance Percy!' the rebel men-at-arms and remaining archers left their position on the ridge and surged forward to engage the royal army. According to Walsingham, the attack was aimed in a 'mad career towards one person, the king, counting him as worth 10,000 others'. Hotspur and the earl of Douglas were at the forefront of this attack, both being singled out for their unparalleled courage and clarity of purpose. Not all the rebels had such focus and many on the east of the battle broke off in pursuit of the fleeing royalists. Others with an eye for plunder and profit joined in with the ransacking of the royal baggage train and did not return to the battlefield.

The Fastolf sword is a remarkable survivor of an edged weapon type common at the beginning of the 15th century. The sword has long had an association with Sir John Fastolf, whose character was twisted to become the Falstaff of Shakespeare's *Henry IV, Part I*. (Norwich Castle Museum, NWHCM: 1955.38)

The Percy assault on the king's person was designed to bring the battle to a swift conclusion, and was based upon a sound assessment of the likely means by which victory could be achieved. Once the king was dead, the royal army would almost certainly lose morale, collapse and flee. Such an outcome would also probably end with the death or capture of the prince and the other important noblemen arrayed against the rebels. The clash of the men-at-arms when the armies met was fierce. Percy calls were answered by cries of 'St George!' from the royal side and the king himself was called upon to fight for his life in the mêlée.

With such a focus upon the centre of the battle the flanks of the rebel army, in particular, were dangerously exposed. Prince Henry now led his battle in an attack against the Percy vanguard, possibly commanded by the earl of Worcester. As the two sides closed together for combat, it is possible that some men-at-arms chose to raise or remove their visors for better visibility and to allow them to breathe freely during the extraordinary physical demands of close-quarters fighting. Although potentially beneficial in the mêlée, this action made them extremely vulnerable to arrows. Many archers would have accompanied more heavily equipped men-at-arms into the fray, swapping their bows for swords, knives and other handheld weapons when required. Until their last arrow was loosed, however, they were free to shoot at the enemy over and between the heads of their compatriots. Others may have been employed as marksmen, intended to pick off specific targets or men-at-arms who showed signs of vulnerability or exposed flesh.

At this point, if not earlier during the opening archery storm, Prince Henry was shot in the face by an arrow which penetrated deep into the flesh and embedded itself in the bone of his skull next to his nose. The sources tell us that the prince remained on the battlefield, leading his men from the front. According to Edward Hall: 'The prince Henry that daie holpe muche

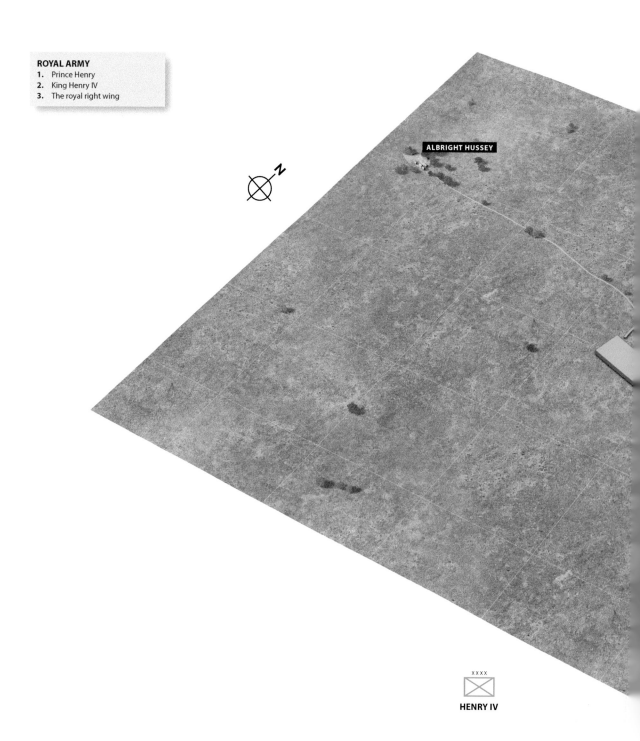

ROYAL ARMY
1. Prince Henry
2. King Henry IV
3. The royal right wing

ALBRIGHT HUSSEY

xxxx

HENRY IV

EVENTS

1. Hotspur has the best of the archery exchange as the skill of the Cheshire and Welsh bowmen overcomes that of the royal archers.

2. A large number of men from Henry IV's vanguard begin to flee in disorder, shaken by the casualties inflicted by the rebel archers. Some raid the royal baggage train as they leave the battlefield, taking the horses and valuables of their fellows with them.

3. Some of those in the rebel army pursue the fleeing royalists. Others join in the looting already taking place amongst the royal baggage train.

4. To kill the king and end the battle quickly, the rebels concentrate their attack on Henry IV's position.

5. With the hand-to-hand fighting in the centre of the battlefield so fierce, the king withdraws from the front line on the advice of the earl of Dunbar.

6. Prince Henry launches a counter-attack. It is probably at this point, as the men-at-arms near each other, that the Prince is wounded in the face by an arrow.

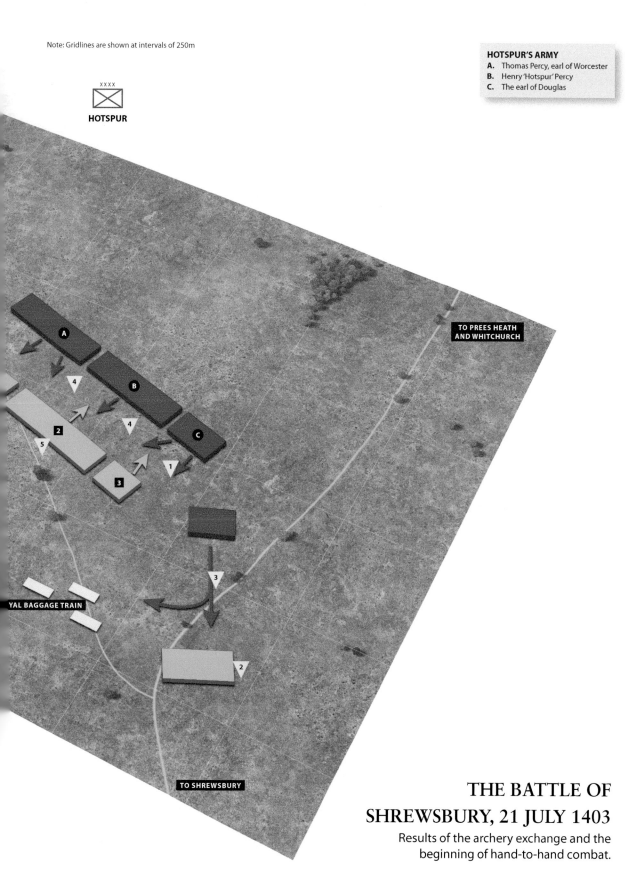

Note: Gridlines are shown at intervals of 250m

HOTSPUR

TO PREES HEATH
AND WHITCHURCH

YAL BAGGAGE TRAIN

TO SHREWSBURY

THE BATTLE OF
SHREWSBURY, 21 JULY 1403
Results of the archery exchange and the
beginning of hand-to-hand combat.

PRINCE HENRY IS SHOT IN THE FACE BY AN ARROW WHILE LEADING AN ATTACK ON THE REBEL VANGUARD (PP. 66–67)

Thomas Walsingham provides us with the detail that allows us to imagine the moment during the battle of Shrewsbury when Prince Henry was shot in the face with an arrow: 'Meanwhile the destruction dealt by the arrows, which were flying like a hailstorm from both sides, was very great. The Prince, then fighting his first battle, was shot in the face by an arrow; boy though he was, he did not falter, but with courage beyond his years, disregarding his wounds, cheered on his troops to vengeance.'

Other accounts, such as *Hall's Chronicle*, agree that the prince fought on despite his injury, 'never ceasing either to fight where the battle was strongest, or to encourage his men where their hearts were most daunted'. This picture shows the moment at which Henry was wounded, the prince recoiling against the impact of the arrow penetrating his head **(1)**. Sir John Stanley, steward of the prince's household, is shown supporting his master **(2)** as a Percy archer draws his bow to

shoot another arrow towards the pair **(3)**. Stanley himself was sorely wounded during the battle by an arrow in the throat. Another man who may have been close to the prince during the battle was Sir John Massey of Puddington **(4)**, a staunch Lancastrian supporter who had earlier served under Hotspur in Wales. Prince Henry's own white swan pennant can be seen flying above him, while further afield the standards of the earls of Warwick and Arundel **(5)** can be seen closing on the rebel ranks. Against them can be seen the earl of Worcester, flanked by Sir Hugh Browe and Sir William Stanley **(6)**. Another man who had recently defected from the Shrewsbury garrison was Sir John Pulle **(7)** shown with spear in hand. Although it is not known whether these men directly faced the prince during the battle, such a scenario would have undoubtedly resulted in the type of ferocious hand-to-hand fighting well described in the sources.

his father, for although he wer sore wouded in the face with an arow, yet he neuer ceased ether to fight where the battail was moste strongest, or to courage his men where their hertes was moste danted.'

With such a wound we must doubt whether the prince possessed the ability to carry on fighting in person. The arrow and its shaft could not be removed and the shock and pain of the wound would have been excruciating. Rather than fighting himself, it is possible that the prince remained on the field amidst his men, encouraging them and 'cheering them on to vengeance', in the words of the *Dieulacres Chronicle*. This, given his condition, would have been a considerable act of bravery and fortitude, guaranteed to boost the morale of his men and spur them on to fight on his behalf. In the prince's immediate absence it is probable that a more experienced soldier, perhaps already acting as Henry's mentor during the battle, now took on personal command. The prince would have been surrounded by men whom he knew and trusted. For example, Sir John Stanley was a proven military man and was serving as steward of the prince's household. He had fought with Henry during his recent Welsh campaigns and would have been known to the fighting men contracted to serve in Wales. It is also possible that great magnates, such as the earls of Arundel or Warwick, were also fighting by the prince in the battle. With Henry incapacitated, it fell to men such as these to organize and lead the attack. Even with their leader injured, this attack soon proved to be highly successful and their momentum quickly began to force the Percy vanguard to retreat and compress itself against the rebel centre.

In these conditions the hand-to-hand combat would have been fierce. The men in the prince's battle would have been keen to maximize their initial success while the rebels would have fought desperately to avoid disaster. The bloody encounter was worsened by the gathering dusk. In medieval battles the combat was often allowed to ebb and flow. Periods of sustained effort were interspersed by small lulls that allowed individual combatants to rest while their compatriots continued the fight. At Shrewsbury, however, the combat was conducted at the end of the day and constricted to an unusually short timeframe. Walsingham says the entire battle lasted a mere two hours, a span that prevented any chance of rest for either side.

Nowhere was the fighting more intense than around the king himself, whose position was advertised by his banner which acted as a beacon to all those involved. According to many of the sources, Hotspur and Douglas were at the forefront of the attack. *The English Chronicle* says that: '[Seeing] his men faste yslayne, he [Hotspur] preesed into the bataille with 30 men of armes and made a layne in medull off the hoste till he comme to the kynges banner.'

The Lyle Bascinet in the collection of the Royal Armouries is a North Italian example of the helmet form most common among men-at-arms in the late 14th and early 15th century. The skull is forged from one piece of steel with a separate attached visor. These helmets provided excellent protection against arrows but afforded limited vision to the wearer. (Royal Armouries, IV.470)

Archers often went into battle with far less protection than more heavily armoured men-at-arms. This late 14th-century manuscript illustration shows archers in battle without the advantage of plate armour. (British Library, Ms. Royal 6 E VI, f. 183)

HENRY IV'S STANDARD-BEARER IS CUT DOWN BY THE EARL OF DOUGLAS (PP. 70–71)

The hand-to-hand fighting around King Henry was the fiercest across the whole battlefield. According to Walsingham: 'Henry Percy … and the Earl of Douglas … scorned the series ranks of his [Henry IV's] men at arms, and, stirring up all their strength, turned their arms against one person, the king himself. They reckoned he was worth ten thousand men… When the earl of Dunbar perceived their intention, he withdrew the king from his position at the front to prevent his being found by those seeking his life.'

Hall's Chronicle, however, provides a more heroic account of the king's actions: 'The king, crying "Saint George, victory!" broke the array and entered into the battle of his enemies and fought fiercely, and ventured so far into the battle, that the earl of Douglas struck him down and slew sir Water Blount.'

In this picture the earl of Douglas (1) is shown slaying the king's standard-bearer with a mighty blow of his poleaxe. Sir Walter Blount (2) is shown stretching out his arm in an attempt to stop the standard falling to the ground. A short distance away, Henry IV is shown being warned by George Dunbar of the peril of his current situation (3). Other accounts do not include the detail that Henry temporarily withdrew, instead saying that he fought on and killed some 36 of his enemies with his own hand. Behind the king, Sir Robert Goushill, who had been knighted on the day of the battle, reaches out with his weapon attempting to strike at the earl of Douglas (4). At the bottom of the picture lies the corpse of Edmund, earl of Stafford (5). According to the *Dieulacres Chronicle*, he was killed by an arrow while leading the front rank of the king's battle.

It was at this time, if not during the archery duel, that the earl of Stafford was killed. Another of the slain was the king's standard-bearer, according to some accounts, by either Hotspur or Douglas themselves. Later sources, such as Holinshed, suggest that the royal standard was held by Sir Walter Blount, with the *Brut* reporting that Blount was killed wearing the 'Kynges cot Armure'. Usk and Hall also say that up to three others were 'appareled in the kynges suite and clothyng'. These descriptions heavily suggest that the king employed decoys, wearing the king's arms, designed to conceal his true location on the battlefield. Before the battle of Poitiers in 1356, the French king John II (also known as John the Good) is said to have deployed 19 decoys in the French royal arms. Despite this precedent, and the obvious purpose of disguising Henry's own person, the possibility of decoys should not be so readily accepted. For their disguises to be effective and believable, they would have had to be arrayed in armour and clothing of a quality expected of the king. Although Henry is certain to have had many suits of armour in his possession, it is more questionable whether the king had such a number available at such short notice. More crucially, the king acted as a focal point and figurehead on the battlefield to his men. During the fighting they would look to him to gather the assurance and confidence they needed to continue the fight. The death of a decoy risked his men mistaking it for the death of the king himself. If this error had gained wide acceptance among his army, the resulting confusion and panic would have likely resulted in an immediate and wide-scale rout, potentially leading to the very death the decoys were designed to prevent. Another reason to doubt the story is that it seems to originate in the writings of Adam Usk. Although Usk is often an excellent source, his critical attitude towards Henry is well established. His exile from England in January 1403 also means that he was reliant on second-hand accounts for his description of the battle. It is possible, therefore, that Usk was mistaken or that he deliberately chose to diminish the king's bravery during the battle. Following Usk, the story became popular and is present in many of the later sources. In Shakespeare's version of the battle, when Hotspur informs Douglas that 'the king hath many marching in his coats', the gruff Scotsman declares, in typically brusque fashion, that he will annihilate 'the entire royal wardrobe'.

The death of Henry's standard-bearer is testimony to how close Henry came to losing his own life. According to Walsingham, the earl of Dunbar perceived the rebel intent and withdrew the king from his original position to one of comparative safety. This proved fortuitous, as the squire who carried Henry's shield was overthrown and the king's banner was hurled down and ripped to shreds. Other chronicles praise the king for the feats of arms he performed during the battle. The *Dieulacres Chronicle* says that Henry fought on through the onslaught with an axe and caused great carnage among his enemies. Hall adds that he personally slew 36 of the rebel number but was, at one point, struck down by the earl of Douglas.

This was the deciding moment of the battle. The flight of the royal vanguard had proved to be indecisive and the main body of the king's army was standing firm with their king. The success of the prince, however, had made matters desperate for the rebels, whose own pursuit of King Henry became more frenzied as a result. When the royal standard fell the rebels were encouraged, letting out shouts of jubilation, but soon after, at the height of the battle, Hotspur was killed while still pressing into the thick of the action.

ROYAL ARMY
1. Prince Henry
2. King Henry IV
3. The royal right wing

ALBRIGHT HUSSEY

XXXX

HENRY IV

 EVENTS

1. The attack launched by Prince Henry is successful. The Percy vanguard is forced back and trapped between the prince's division and the men of their own centre.

2. Hotspur launches a final assault on the king's person, in which attempt he is cut down by an unknown hand. The mêlée combat has become so chaotic that Hotspur's death is not immediately known.

3. When royal shouts concerning Hotspur's death go unanswered, the rebels realize the battle is lost and begin to flee. The royal pursuit is curtailed by the gathering dusk and the king's calls for an end to the bloodshed.

Note: Gridlines are shown at intervals of 250m

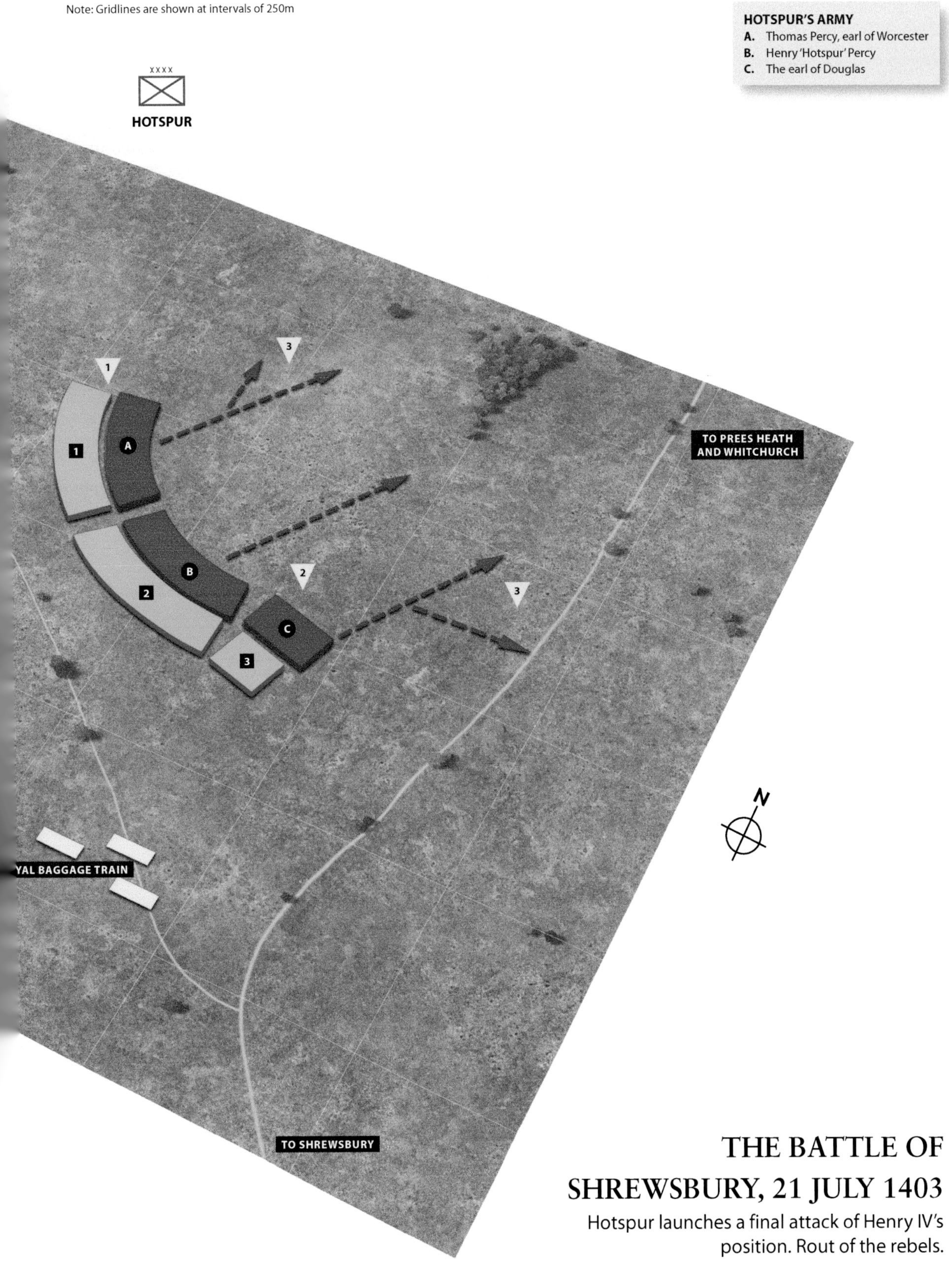

HOTSPUR'S ARMY
A. Thomas Percy, earl of Worcester
B. Henry 'Hotspur' Percy
C. The earl of Douglas

XXXX
HOTSPUR

TO PREES HEATH
AND WHITCHURCH

N

YAL BAGGAGE TRAIN

TO SHREWSBURY

THE BATTLE OF
SHREWSBURY, 21 JULY 1403
Hotspur launches a final attack of Henry IV's
position. Rout of the rebels.

The circumstances of Hotspur's death are uncertain, with one plausible tradition suggesting that he was killed by an arrow as he raised his visor to survey the field; other less likely sources credit the king with killing Hotspur personally. More reputable sources suggest that Hotspur was killed almost alone after penetrating too far into royal lines. There, still fighting manfully, he was cut down surrounded by his enemies. It is likely that in the chaos, Hotspur's death was not immediately widely known among either side. Walsingham records the uncertainty vividly: 'Henry Percy was slain, by whose hand it is doubtful, nor were his soldiers aware of it, thinking that he had either seized the king's person, or doubtless, perished in the attempt.'

Accordingly, in order to encourage their own men, some of the rebels took up the war-cry, 'Henry Percy King!', causing great consternation among the royal army. Although Hotspur lay dead, this still presented a great danger to the king that he, too, would be slain in the confusion. In defiance of the rebel cries, the king led a return shout of 'Henry Percy is dead!' that was soon echoed among the royal army. It must have soon become clear to all nearby, waiting in ghoulish anticipation, that no reply was forthcoming. This could mean only one thing – Hotspur had truly been slain.

It is testament to Hotspur's fame that, despite his status as a rebel, several of the sources lament the death of the 'the flower and glory of chivalry of Christendom.' With Hotspur dead, the rebel cause was lost and many in his army turned to flight. The rout was always the deadliest period of a battle as the victors were overcome with bloodlust and looked to take revenge on their defeated opponents with their backs turned. Unlike battles on foreign soil, there was little advantage in taking prisoners for ransom as the rebels were traitors deserving of death. This probably ensured that none but the rebel leaders, rounded up specifically for the king's own judgement, received any mercy on the battlefield. Among those targeted would have been the rebel Cheshire knights, esquires and archers who had inflicted so much damage to the royal army. Fortunately for the rebels, the dark had the effect of preventing an organized pursuit. In other areas of the battle more distant from Hotspur's death there was great confusion. Walsingham records: 'Very many of the combatants on both sides struggled with such obstinacy that when night came on they did not know which side had won; and they sank down in all directions a chance-medley of weary, wounded, bruised, and bleeding men.'

At this stage, the battlefield must have extended over several square miles as small groups of men broke off in their own direction. Any further pursuit was called off by the king who, according to the *Dieulacres Chronicle*, removed his helmet and shouted out often, 'Do not kill any more of my people'.

Most of the rebels fled north up the Whitchurch Road in the direction from which they had arrived two days earlier. Others, indifferent to their previous affiliation and trusting in the anonymity of night, took to despoiling and looting the bodies of the dead and wounded. Walsingham records the particular story of Sir Robert Goushill who fought on the king's side and had been knighted on the day of the battle. Having been sorely wounded, Goushill retired from the front lines seeking refuge beneath a hedgerow. Later, his servant found him and recognized his master by the heraldic badges engraved on his dented armour. The servant had cowardly run away during the combat but was now returning 'like a grave-robber, after the manner of such folk, to plunder the bodies of the slain'. After helping his master out of the armour that was preventing its wearer from breathing freely, Goushill handed the servant a signet ring and 60 marks from his purse. The ring was supposed to be handed to the knight's wife while the money was to be used for his sustenance while recuperating, or, if he should die, to be kept by the servant for his service. However, rather than fulfil his master's

The originally fine alabaster tomb of Sir Robert Goushill in the Church of St Michael in Hoveringham, Staffordshire. The extraordinary account of Sir Robert's death is vividly described in the *Annales Henrici Quarti*. (Author's photograph)

wishes, the servant withdrew a dagger and plunged it repeatedly into Robert's chest 'till he saw him quite dead'. He then looted the remaining armour and badges of rank, including collar, jewels and rings, and made off, leaving the stripped corpse of his master where it lay. The crime did not go unpunished, however, as it was witnessed by another man who later recounted the event to the duchess of Norfolk. The murderer was caught and convicted by the evidence of the stolen goods and received the 'punishment that he deserved'. As the dark fell, similarly unhappy scenes must have been played out across the battlefield as the tortured cries of the wounded and dying sounded out in the night air.

THE AFTERMATH

CASUALTIES

One fact upon which all the chroniclers agreed was the exceptional number of casualties sustained. The *Brut* records the battle was 'was the heviest, and unkyndest and sorest … that ever was before that tyme in Englond'. Of particular note was the unusually high number of nobles, knights and men-at-arms among the slain. This can probably be attributed to the opening archery contest and the peculiarly ferocious hand-to-hand fighting among the men-at-arms. The short time in which the battle took place also had a significant effect, as both sides sought to conclude the combat before the remaining daylight faded.

Of the commanders named in the chronicles, two – Hotspur and Stafford – died on the field, while a third, Prince Henry, was seriously wounded. The king himself also came perilously close to losing his life. There is no reason to suppose that the high mortality rate among the commanders misrepresents the wider situation among the other combatants, some 50 of whom can be named specifically among the casualties. Several chronicles give the figure of 200 Cheshire knights and squires killed. This number is likely to be nearly accurate, as the more important corpses would have to be identified and counted among the dead. Those ordered to perform this macabre task were, no doubt, aided by the surcoats and heraldic badges decorating the armour of the slain. A smaller figure for the fallen is supplied by the *Dieulacres Chronicle* which says that 28 knights were killed in the royal army, compared to only eight for the rebels. This discrepancy, if accurate, may reflect the desperate nature of the fighting around the king and the sacrifice of Henry's men in ensuring his safety at the cost of their own lives. It might also indicate the success of Hotspur's archers at the beginning of the battle.

The casualty rate among the lower orders was also high. Usk provides the figure of 16,000 total dead but such a number seems

James William Edmund Doyle's illustration of Hotpur's death depicts the event in serene style, with Percy surrounded by his men, including the earl of Douglas. In all probability, Hotspur's death occurred in far more chaotic circumstances, during the last assault on Henry IV's person. When knowledge of his death became widespread the rebel army collapsed. (Author's collection)

to be grossly exaggerated and may be a scribal error, based upon the 1,600 given in the *Eulogium*. The same figure of 1,600 is given as the number of royal dead in both Hall and Hayward, with the same authors reporting the rebel dead as between 5,000 and 6,000. Walsingham states that 3,000 yeomen and squires were wounded in Henry IV's army and laments that many of these later died after succumbing to their wounds.

Walsingham's figures for the total participants and number of injured reveal a casualty rate of over 20 per cent among the royal army, rising to nearly 30 per cent if the 4,000 men he cites as quitting the field, following the opening archery exchange, are excluded. Such a high figure, up to one third of the participants, is an unusual, but not unprecedented total when compared to the estimated numbers of casualties on several other medieval battlefields. Strikingly, however, Walsingham's figures only relate to the royal army and the figure for the rebel side would, unarguably, have been larger.

Another indication of the high number of deaths is the reference to of the mass grave dug for the slain that is mentioned in many of the chronicle accounts. This grisly detail, often neglected in other battle accounts, was clearly deemed worthy of particular note. The highest number is given by the Wigmore Chronicler, who says that 3,460 were buried in a pit 100ft long, 24ft wide and 12ft deep. The Durham Chronicler gives a lower number of 2,291, *Dieulacres* 1,847 and the *Brut* 1,100.

This statue of Henry IV is placed above the east window of Battlefield Church. It is one of the few portrayals of Henry to survive from the time of his reign. (Author's photograph)

THE LEADING REBELS

After the battle had concluded, several of the leading rebels were captured. Thomas Percy, earl of Worcester was taken on the field with Sir Richard Venables and Sir Richard Vernon. Some sources also say that the earl of Douglas was taken after being wounded in the groin. Hall provides a more imaginative version, reporting that the earl was captured after falling from the crag of a nearby mountain, perhaps the Wrekin, through which accident he lost one of his testicles. His captor, James Haryngton, later received the generous reward of an annuity of 100 marks. Douglas, being a foreigner not subject to the English Crown and so free from the taint of rebellion, gained extensive praise among the chroniclers for his heroic role in the battle. Walsingham, for instance, extolled his courage and endurance, saying that if the other rebels had fought with equal skill, disaster would have befallen the English nation. Shrewsbury, however, was now the second time in less than a year that Douglas had been taken captive by an English adversary.

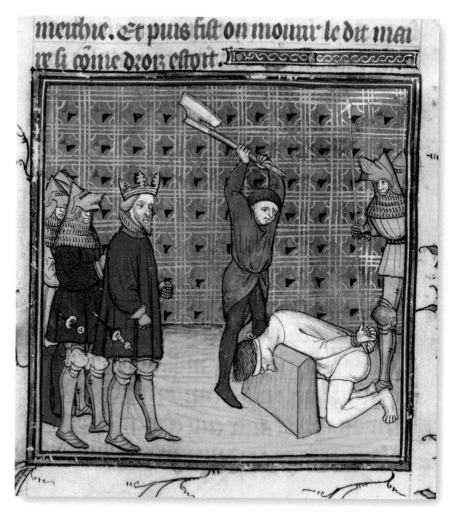

When Hotspur's corpse was recovered and shown to Henry IV, the king is supposed to have wept at the sight. Initially, the body was handed over to Hotspur's kinsman Thomas Neville, Lord Furnival, who had it buried with full Christian rites in Whitchurch. The following day, however, the king had the body disinterred and returned to Shrewsbury for ignominious treatment. For this act, a later church writer hostile to Henry lambasted him as 'a blood-thirsty beast, still thirsting for his blood'. The truth, however, is that Henry could not afford to let such an act of rebellion go seemingly unpunished. Another factor that caused Henry concern were the rumours, quickly spread, that Hotspur had survived. In order to end these whispers, and to make an example to others, the king had Hotspur's body duly set up between two millstones in the city marketplace, next to the pillory, and guarded by armed men so that all passers-by might bear witness. The next day the body was beheaded, quartered and the parts dispatched to the mayors of London, Bristol, Newcastle and Chester. The head was sent to York and, by tradition, set above Micklegate Bar.

Worcester, like Henry IV, is supposed to have wept upon seeing his nephew's body. According to Walsingham, the king wished to spare Thomas's life but was persuaded against this by his friends, incensed by the rebel's conduct and the thought that his treachery could go unpunished.

Accordingly, Worcester was given a brief hearing and, along with Venables and Vernon, swiftly found guilty, with all being executed soon after. The accounts of William Banastre, sheriff of the city, provide a fascinating but gruesome record of his expenses incurred in sending the heads of the rebels across the country. The heads were preserved with wax, salt and resin and put in sacks containing cloves, cumin, anise and other spices. Worcester's head was sent to the capital and set upon London Bridge 'as long as it can last' while the heads of the Cheshire lords were sent to Chester as a warning to the local community. The total cost of this undertaking, including the transport of Hotspur's remains, was £13 15s.

After being displayed for a few months, the remains of Hotspur and Worcester were taken down. On 3 November 1403 Henry IV granted Elizabeth Mortimer, Hotspur's wife, his remains for burial, the location of which remains uncertain. Worcester's head was removed from London Bridge by the order of the king on 18 December 1403 and was trusted to the care of John Clifford and Thomas de Burgh, who took it under order to Shrewsbury Abbey. There the head was reunited with the earl's body and buried with the permission of the abbot.

THE CHESHIRE REBELS AND ROYAL REWARDS

Soon after the battle, messages were sent across the country to inform the people of the failure of the rebellion and the safety of the king. Receipts for a total of £5 10s for messengers' expenses indicate the importance that the king attached to disseminating the news. With the rising defeated and its leaders either dead or captured, the king now had to decide on a course of action against the remaining rebels and the localities most heavily implicated. According to the *Brut*, the king sent a courier to ask the advice of Sir John Stanley, steward of the prince's household. Stanley had been wounded by an arrow in the throat and was in poor mood for compromise. His 'rattelyng' response to what should be done was to 'Burn and slay! Burn and slay!' When the king enquired about Stanley's response, the courier chose to ignore the true response and reported that Stanley had advised the king to 'take them to grace'. Accordingly, 'al that wold ask grace that were taken had grace and forgyvenes'. According to the *Brut*, not all the king's men agreed, and many proceeded into Cheshire to loot and despoil the country.

On 9 November, a general pardon was granted to all those who had rebelled in Cheshire, followed by a similar pardon granted on the 22nd to all those in Northumberland, Cumberland, Westmorland and Yorkshire who sued for pardon before the Epiphany, 6 January 1404. The *Dieulacres Chronicle* says that this general pardon was granted by the king, more out of fear than love. For Henry, the experience of having two important border counties rising against his rule was a reminder of his precarious hold on the throne. At his coronation, he had promised to rule justly and by his own means. However, his rule had been beset by rebellion and his poor financial situation often forced him to renege on his coronation oath. Once the leaders of the rebellion had been punished, Henry's policy towards the remaining rebels therefore became conciliatory rather than retributive. This lenient attitude was intended to appease further discontent and to convert past enemies to his cause. Cheshire was also an important bulwark in the defence of the realm, and its history of supplying high-quality soldiers to royal armies may have prevented Henry from wanting to cripple this resource any further. This consideration was especially important in 1403, as the Welsh uprising threatened to spiral out of control. Another factor that allowed Henry to be temperate in his dealings was that many of the most recalcitrant rebels to his rule were now dead. These included men who had possessed the ability to recruit large personal followings against the king, such as Sir John Massey of Tatton and Sir Hugh Browe. The names of around 20 high-ranking members of county society who died fighting against the king are known. In addition, 31 inquisitions *post mortem* which record the death and estates of lower-ranking men survive. Many of this number are likely to have fought with Hotspur.

Large numbers of the rebels who survived the battle got away with paying a light fine, while others escaped punishment completely. For example, Sir Thomas Grosvenor was pardoned on 15 August, and excused any forfeiture of his lands and goods while another rebel, Richard Massey, was pardoned on payment of the small sum of £5. Some prominent rebels even returned to positions of responsibility soon after, with three – Sir William Stanley, Sir John Poole and John Litherland – being awarded the position of 'conservators and guardians' of the Wirral as early as 25 August. Significantly, their duties included the protection of the coast against the Welsh rebels. Only rebels who exhibited peculiar defiance were spared pardon. The lands of one John Leftwich were granted to William Kirby after he failed to submit to the king. Others, such as John Kynaston, earned their disgrace by siding with Glyndŵr. Henry's extraordinary generosity to the defeated rebels, however, is again demonstrated by the fact that both these men eventually gained pardon in return for their submission. Both were rehabilitated and received their

Shrewsbury Abbey lies outside the centre of the town, near to the English Bridge. Thomas Percy's body was buried in the building following his execution. In December 1403, King Henry ordered the abbot to allow Worcester's head to be laid to rest alongside his other remains. (Author's collection)

The Abbey Church Shrewsbury.

Wressle Castle had been built by Thomas Percy in the 1390s in a modern and luxurious style. In 1403 Henry IV granted it to his new queen, Joan of Navarre. (By courtesy of Wressle Castle)

confiscated lands and properties back. Henry also showed generosity to the relatives of those killed on the rebel side. Six widows, whose husbands' lands had been forfeited to the Crown, are known to have been compensated. For example, Joyce, widow of William de Legh, was granted a percentage of his forfeited goods to the value of £24.

With their defeat at Shrewsbury, the anti-Lancastrian faction in Cheshire evaporated. The conclusiveness of the battle, the personal bravery exhibited by the king and the demonstration to contemporary minds of God's will in favouring the Lancastrians, all contributed to ensuring that the memory of Richard II was finally laid to rest. The continued war against Glyndŵr helped to focus attention against a single common and external enemy, while Prince Henry's presence and success in Wales during the following decade encouraged previous foes into the royal fold. The measured attitude adopted by Henry IV towards the county ensured that Cheshire remained loyal to Henry for the rest of his reign and did not join any of the subsequent rebellions against his rule.

The leniency Henry showed the defeated rebels did not mean that those on his own side went unrewarded. Several grants and promotions occurred almost immediately. Richard Beauchamp, earl of Warwick, was inducted into the Order of the Garter for his role in the battle, an event later celebrated in the Beauchamp Pageant. During the following weeks and months, more substantial rewards of property forfeited by the rebels were given to the king's supporters. Chief among the beneficiaries were the nobility who had fought in the battle, while the greatest rewards came from the properties and offices of state forfeited by Hotspur and Worcester. The prince was given all the silver vessels formally belonging to the earl of Worcester 'in whosesoever hands they can be found' while the earl of Dunbar also received several Percy properties, rights and other goods. An indication of the splendour and value of such belongings can be ascertained from the description of the contents of Thomas Percy's house in Bishopsgate: 'a coverlet of *baudekyn* [silk brocade], partly red and black, and bound with red *bokeram* [fine cotton cloth] value 30s; a *coverlit* of *satyngrounde* [satin bedspread] with white swans, value 4 marks; and 2 *materaces* of green *taffeta* [silk mattresses], value 26s 8d.' The queen was granted Wressle Castle, built by Worcester in modern and fashionable style, while other beneficiaries included Prince John, the earl of Kent, numerous other noblemen, royal knights, squires and servants. Ralph Neville, the Percy's most powerful northern rival, received the custody of Berwick and Bamburgh, ensuring his ascendancy of the border in the future.

SUBSEQUENT ACTION

Although Henry IV had won the battle, there were several situations that still needed his attention. One of these was the continued Welsh revolt and the security of the border counties. On 23 July, the king appointed the earl of Arundel and four others 'to resist the rebels if they presume to invade the marches, and to make war against and destroy them'. The appointment was presumably made as the prince, recovering from his injuries, was not able to proceed himself.

The arrow that had struck the prince remained lodged in his face. To remove it the royal physician John Bradmore was called in to devise a method of extraction. After a few days, during which the prince must have been in acute physical discomfort, despite being treated with herb and plant extracts, a solution was found. The operation began by removing the shaft of the arrow but, as Bradmore wrote, 'the head of the aforesaid arrow remained in the furthermost past of the bone of the skull for the depth of six inches'. This problem had been anticipated, as arrows were often designed to break upon impact to impede removal. Bradmore had therefore designed a custom tool to remove the head. This device was fashioned of small hollow tongs the width of an arrow, through which ran a screw. To remove the arrowhead the tongs were designed to penetrate the wound and enter the internal socket of the arrowhead. The screw would then be tightened to expand the tongs and grip the arrowhead by friction. By 'moving it to and fro, little by little' Bradmore was then able to successfully extract the arrowhead from the prince's skull. Once the wound was clear it was cleansed, using a syringe filled with white wine, before being filled with wads of flax soaked in a purifying solution of white bread, barley flour, honey and turpentine oil. Twenty days were required for the wound to heal with the purifying wads shortened each day. After this process was complete a 'dark ointment' was applied to reduce the scarring.

While the prince recovered, the king turned his attention to stamping out the last remnants of the rebellion. The earl of Northumberland remained at large, reportedly with a substantial armed following. On 22 July Henry ordered Ralph Neville and a number of other northern lords to proceed against the armed 'traitors' and, should Northumberland be captured, to bring him before the king in person. Henry set out from Shrewsbury soon after with a substantial force to counter Northumberland in person. He reached Stafford on the 25th, Nottingham on the 29th and, by 4 August, had reached Pontefract Castle in Yorkshire. On the way, Henry sent out a stream of orders, one of which, sent upon his arrival at Pontefract, ordered the sheriffs of the city of York, Yorkshire and Northumberland to prevent spoliation of the tenants of the Percys. Another letter, sent on the 6th, anticipated Scottish action and gave powers to Sir Robert Umfraville and Sir Gerard Heron to treat for a truce with Scotland, in order to prevent them from exploiting the death of Hotspur and the uncertain situation on the northern border.

Aftermath of the battle

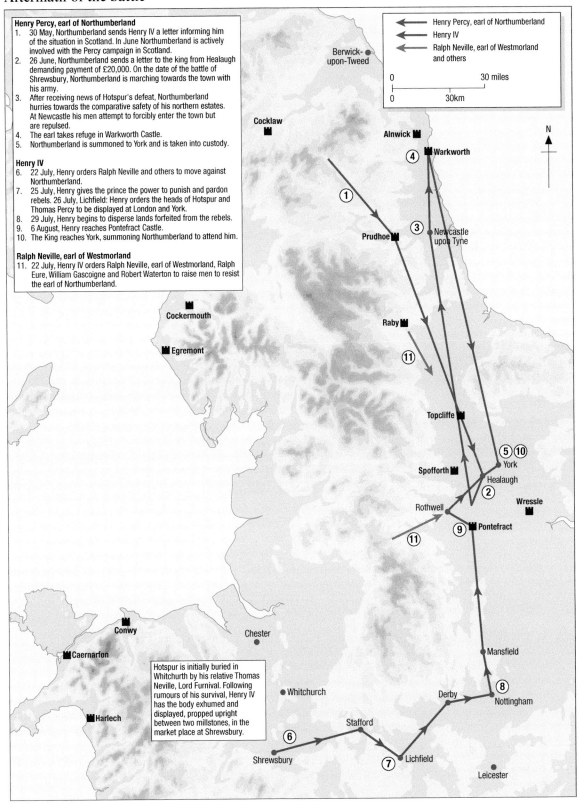

Henry Percy, earl of Northumberland
1. 30 May, Northumberland sends Henry IV a letter informing him of the situation in Scotland. In June Northumberland is actively involved with the Percy campaign in Scotland.
2. 26 June, Northumberland sends a letter to the king from Healaugh demanding payment of £20,000. On the date of the battle of Shrewsbury, Northumberland is marching towards the town with his army.
3. After receiving news of Hotspur's defeat, Northumberland hurries towards the comparative safety of his northern estates. At Newcastle his men attempt to forcibly enter the town but are repulsed.
4. The earl takes refuge in Warkworth Castle.
5. Northumberland is summoned to York and is taken into custody.

Henry IV
6. 22 July, Henry orders Ralph Neville and others to move against Northumberland.
7. 25 July, Henry gives the prince the power to punish and pardon rebels. 26 July, Lichfield: Henry orders the heads of Hotspur and Thomas Percy to be displayed at London and York.
8. 29 July, Henry begins to disperse lands forfeited from the rebels.
9. 6 August, Henry reaches Pontefract Castle.
10. The King reaches York, summoning Northumberland to attend him.

Ralph Neville, earl of Westmorland
11. 22 July, Henry IV orders Ralph Neville, earl of Westmorland, Ralph Eure, William Gascoigne and Robert Waterton to raise men to resist the earl of Northumberland.

Henry Percy, earl of Northumberland
Henry IV
Ralph Neville, earl of Westmorland and others

0   30 miles
0   30km

N

Berwick-upon-Tweed

Cocklaw

Alnwick
④ Warkworth

③ Newcastle upon Tyne

Prudhoe

Cockermouth

Egremont

Raby

⑪

Topcliffe

Spofforth
⑤ ⑩
York
Healaugh
②
Wressle

Rothwell
⑪
⑨ Pontefract

Conwy

Chester

Caernarfon

Mansfield

Hotspur is initially buried in Whitchurth by his relative Thomas Neville, Lord Furnival. Following rumours of his survival, Henry IV has the body exhumed and displayed, propped upright between two millstones, in the market place at Shrewsbury.

Whitchurch

Derby

⑧ Nottingham

Harlech

Stafford

⑥
Shrewsbury

⑦ Lichfield

Leicester

By tradition, Hotspur's head was set up above Micklegate Bar, one of the many gatehouses in York's city walls. It is possible that the earl of Northumberland passed through this gate for his meeting with Henry IV in August 1403. (Author's photograph)

Once the earl of Northumberland heard news of the battle and of the deaths of his son and brother, and possibly the warning that Westmorland and the king were moving against him, he chose to flee back north rather than continue the rebellion. Rumours of the battle, however, travelled fast and when the earl and his men reached Newcastle they were refused entry. Negotiations took place, after which only the earl and a handful of attendants were allowed to enter. This caused anger among the earl's men left outside the walls who soon attempted to storm the town, only to be forcibly repulsed by the townsmen. Northumberland, realizing that further resistance was futile, disbanded his men and took refuge in his residence at Warkworth Castle.

At Warkworth, Northumberland received word from the king that he was required to come and submit himself to Henry's mercy. If he did so, his life would be spared. The interview took place on 11 August at York, where Hotspur's head now adorned one of the city's gates. At the subsequent talks, Northumberland's culpability and involvement in the rebellion was scrutinized. The earl denied any knowledge of, or participation in, the rising and placed the entirety of the blame on his son and brother. Establishing proof of Northumberland's guilt was difficult, and the earl argued strongly that his armed progress had merely been aimed at promoting peace between the two sides. Although it is tempting to dismiss his testimony as a fabrication designed to save his life, several contemporary sources make it clear that those involved were far from certain about Northumberland's real intentions. The king's own opinions on Northumberland's involvement are unknown, although Walsingham reports that the earl was greeted in a frosty manner 'as a suppliant looking for pardon'. It is likely that Henry had more concerns on his mind than the earl's guilt. Northumberland was now an elderly man without any surviving sons. His heir, Hotspur's son, was only an infant. If the earl was executed, a power vacuum would be created which only the Nevilles could realistically exploit. It is unlikely that Henry, given his recent problems with the Percys, would have wanted to create another over-powerful family on the northern border. Henry had also promised Northumberland his life and the opportunity to plead his case before his peers in parliament.

Until such time as parliament convened, Northumberland was taken into custody and sent to Baginton, Warwickshire, with his castles and properties being placed in the custody of William Heron, Lord Say. Taking control of these fortresses proved difficult, however, as they were garrisoned by men intensely loyal to the Percy family and who proved resistant to the forces sent to take them into royal protection. The garrisons were so intransigent that Northumberland was made to send sealed orders to the garrisons of Warkworth, Alnwick, Berwick, Prudhoe, Langley and

Cockermouth demanding that they abandon their fortifications. It is likely that Northumberland had previously ordered them to be held as a bargaining chip in his negotiations. For the surrender of Berwick, the garrison's leader, Sir William Clifford, made exorbitant demands: a full pardon for himself and his men; back payment from the date of Shrewsbury; that Hotspur's son should be promised his father's full inheritance and that he remain in Clifford's guardianship during his minority.

Parliament met early the next year, in January 1404. Northumberland received widespread support from both lords and commons, was restored to his position and received back all his property held at Henry's coronation in 1399. The only charge Northumberland faced was the minor infraction of breaking the Statute of Liveries. Found guilty, he was sentenced to a fine that was soon remitted by the king. Northumberland renewed his oath of allegiance and was allowed to leave. That the king did not fully trust the earl, however, was shown on the feast of John the Baptist (24 June) when Northumberland was required to hand over his three grandchildren, including Hotspur's son, to Henry IV at Pontefract.

THE TRIPARTITE INDENTURE AND SCROPE'S REBELLION

Although the Percy rebellion had been defeated, opposition to Henry IV remained. In February 1405, the young earl of March and his brother were released by Henry's enemies from their comfortable, but forced, captivity in Windsor Castle and conveyed hurriedly towards the Welsh border. The intention was to hand them over to Edmund Mortimer, the boy's uncle, and Owain Glyndŵr. The possibility that the Mortimer claim to the throne

PONTEFRACT CASTLE.

Pontefract Castle was the site of two momentous events during Henry IV's reign. In February 1400 Richard II died there as a prisoner. In 1404 Northumberland was made to give up his grandchildren to Henry IV at the castle, as surety for his good behaviour. (Author's collection)

could be used to incite further rebellion presented a real danger to Henry IV. In the event, however, the boys were soon recaptured and returned to custody. Later the same month, Mortimer and Glyndŵr sealed a pact of mutual support with the earl of Northumberland in a document that laid out their collective plans once Henry IV had been removed. This document, known as the Tripartite Indenture, confirmed the partition of the kingdom between the conspirators: Mortimer was to receive the bulk of southern England, Glyndŵr an expanded Welsh principality and Northumberland everything from the midlands to Scotland. How developed the plan became, or how seriously it was taken by its creators, is open to speculation. It was never circulated widely and is only mentioned in a single chronicle account. The agreement was never acted upon and subsequent events during the same year combined to make the document a dead letter.

In May 1405, another rebellion broke out in the north while the king was preparing for a campaign in Wales. It began when Northumberland and his ally Thomas, baron Bardolf, gathered 400 men and surrounded the castle at Witton-le-Wear near Bishop Auckland, believing that Ralph Neville, earl of Westmorland, was in residence. Westmorland was now the predominant bastion of royal power in the area and the success of the rebellion depended on his early neutralization. The earl had got wind of the plan, however, and had made an escape to Durham. With this disappointment, Northumberland retreated back to his northern castles, ordering his principal strongholds to be garrisoned and provisioned. At the same time several other risings took place, although the extent of co-ordination is unclear. Two Percy retainers, Sir John Fauconberg and Sir John Colville del Dale, were said to have assembled a substantial force in Cleveland. In York, more serious trouble arose focused around the archbishop, Richard Scrope, and the earl of Norfolk, Thomas Mowbray. On 17 May Scrope galvanized the citizenry of York into action in a public sermon. He and Mowbray drew up a list of grievances that were posted on prominent locations around the city and its environs. By 27 May, a force of some 8000–9000 people had assembled on Shipton Moor, north of the city. Here Scrope and Mowbray waited, perhaps hoping for reinforcements to arrive under Northumberland and Bardolf. Instead, they were confronted, on 29 May, by an army led by Henry IV's third son, Prince John, and the resurgent earl of Westmorland. Negotiations were opened, during which Westmorland assured Scope and Mowbray a redress of their grievances and guaranteed their personal safety once their forces had disbanded. Appropriately mollified, the archbishop and the earl encouraged their supporters to disperse, after which, dispossessed of their armed support, the pair were immediately arrested.

Henry IV soon arrived in the city, having hurried north in furious anger at yet another armed insurrection against his rule. Despite a personal intercession by the archbishop of Canterbury in defence of his fellow archbishop, and the refusal of the Chief Justice to try the prelate, a speedy trial went ahead, at which Scrope and Mowbray were condemned to death. Taken outside the city, the two were executed by beheading. The archbishop's death was especially shocking to contemporaries as never before had an English king sanctioned the execution of a bishop, let alone an archbishop. Miracles attributed to Scrope's intercession began to be reported almost immediately, and Henry's later debilitating skin conditions were often attributed by chroniclers as a punishment from God for his treatment of the prelate.

The battle of Bramham Moor, 1408

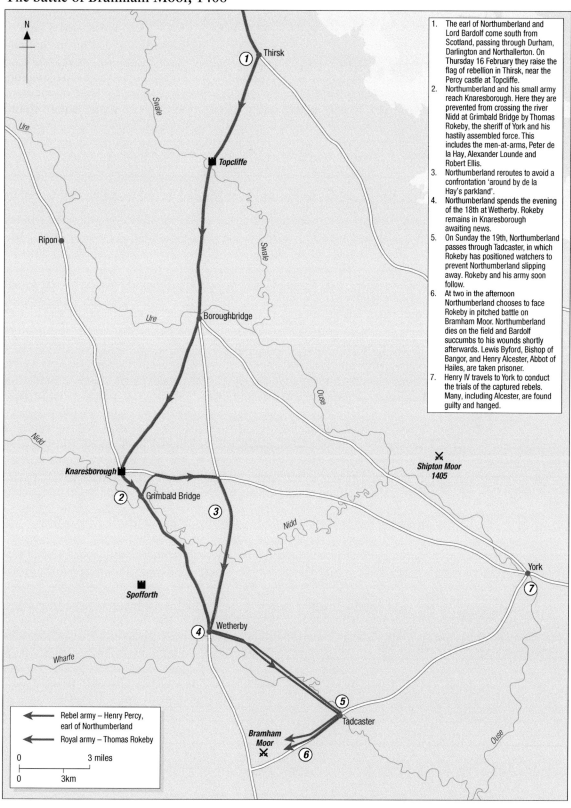

1. The earl of Northumberland and Lord Bardolf come south from Scotland, passing through Durham, Darlington and Northallerton. On Thursday 16 February they raise the flag of rebellion in Thirsk, near the Percy castle at Topcliffe.
2. Northumberland and his small army reach Knaresborough. Here they are prevented from crossing the river Nidd at Grimbald Bridge by Thomas Rokeby, the sheriff of York and his hastily assembled force. This includes the men-at-arms, Peter de la Hay, Alexander Lounde and Robert Ellis.
3. Northumberland reroutes to avoid a confrontation 'around by de la Hay's parkland'.
4. Northumberland spends the evening of the 18th at Wetherby. Rokeby remains in Knaresborough awaiting news.
5. On Sunday the 19th, Northumberland passes through Tadcaster, in which Rokeby has positioned watchers to prevent Northumberland slipping away. Rokeby and his army soon follow.
6. At two in the afternoon Northumberland chooses to face Rokeby in pitched battle on Bramham Moor. Northumberland dies on the field and Bardolf succumbs to his wounds shortly afterwards. Lewis Byford, Bishop of Bangor, and Henry Alcester, Abbot of Hailes, are taken prisoner.
7. Henry IV travels to York to conduct the trials of the captured rebels. Many, including Alcester, are found guilty and hanged.

N

Thirsk

Swale

Ure

Topcliffe

Swale

Ripon

Ure

Boroughbridge

Ouse

Nidd

Shipton Moor
1405

Knaresborough

Grimbald Bridge

Nidd

Spofforth

York

Wetherby

Wharfe

Tadcaster

Ouse

Bramham
Moor

Rebel army – Henry Percy,
earl of Northumberland

Royal army – Thomas Rokeby

0   3 miles

0   3km

NORTHUMBERLAND'S DOWNFALL AND THE BATTLE OF BRAMHAM MOOR

Northumberland's abortive role in Scrope's rebellion could not be ignored and the king soon moved north, subduing Percy castles with the threat, and occasional use, of cannon. Northumberland and Bardolf fled north, finding refuge in Scotland. In their absence they were condemned as traitors, and their lands and goods dispersed among Lancastrian supporters. Northumberland's efforts to procure significant support in Scotland proved fruitless, and in 1406 the two were forced to flee to Wales after receiving warnings that they were about to be betrayed into English hands. After being defeated in a brief skirmish by Edward, Lord Charlton on the border they slipped across the Channel, where they spent several months failing to secure French support for an invasion of England.

In January 1408 during the worst winter in living memory, Northumberland and Bardolf, now back in Scotland, decided to make a last do-or-die attempt at rebellion. Several factors made the timing necessary. The duke of Albany, regent of Scotland during the minority of James I, was seeking peace with England, and during these negotiations, Henry IV would likely demand the two men be handed over to him as prisoners. Numerous other Scottish lords urged them to act without delay. Northumberland may also have received reassurance from England that men in the north would rally to his cause. Moving south with a handful of retainers and a few Scottish mercenaries, the flag of rebellion was raised in Thirsk. Perhaps contrary to Northumberland's expectations, most of the leading gentry and magnates remained aloof, recognizing the cause as doomed. According to Walsingham, however, the rebellion did attract many of the populace 'thinking that everything would turn out as they wished'. The forward advance of Northumberland's army was blocked at Grimbald Bridge, near Knaresborough, by the sheriff of York, Sir Thomas Rokeby, forcing the earl to make a detour via Tadcaster and Bramham Moor where, on 19 February, his force was halted again by Rokeby and brought to battle. Northumberland was said to have preferred to die for his cause rather than be captured. In the resulting battle of Bramham Moor, descriptions of which are perfunctory at best, the rebels were overcome and Northumberland cut down, traditionally as part of a fierce rearguard action. His head was immediately cut off and his corpse stripped. The other commander, Lord Bardolf, was grievously wounded during the battle and died soon afterwards. Several ecclesiastics were taken prisoner, including the bishop of Bangor and abbott of Hailes. As a non-combatant, the former was spared but the latter, due to his arrayal in armour, was hanged. The earl of Northumberland's head, 'handsome with white hair', was impaled upon a lance, carried in public display through the city of London and placed high upon London Bridge.

Northumberland's final attempt to raise rebellion against Henry IV was the action of an increasingly desperate man. The battle of Bramham Moor is commemorated by a marker stone and display panel. (© Mark Anderson/Geograph)

THE BATTLEFIELD TODAY

Unlike other English battles that took place outside the walls of medieval towns, the battlefield at Shrewsbury remains largely intact and unspoilt. Despite many significant changes over the years, the medieval landscape remains largely discernible and can be appreciated, free from excessive modern interference. It is fortunate that the site of the battle remains in active use as farmland and it remains possible to understand the terrain of the battlefield, appreciate the rationale of the participants and place the known sequence of events within the physical landscape.

The open field system in existence at the time of the battle has been swept away, replaced with hedges that break the visitor's gaze as they look across the battlefield. The imposition of modern infrastructure has also had some effect, most obviously in the existence of the railway line opened in 1858 on the east side of the battlefield. The growth of Shrewsbury has also had an impact, and modern industrial estates now border the battlefield to the south, disrupting the medieval sightline between the battlefield and the town.

The site is contained by the A49 to the east and A528 to the west, just over a mile distant. The 1675 road map of the Scottish cartographer John Ogilvy shows that the course of each road has remained largely static since that date, and it is likely both follow a course long established by 1403. The A49 continues past the battlefield to Whitchurch, Chester and the north-west, with the A528 taking a route towards Ellesmere, Wrexham and North Wales. Both would have been used during the Shrewsbury campaign, when Hotspur's army arrived at the scene and as soldiers fled following the conclusion of the battle. A new dual carriageway, the A1524 Battlefield Link Road, was completed in 1998 and forms the southern boundary of the site.

The interior of Battlefield Church with its magnificent hammerbeam roof and reredos, installed in renovations by S. Pountney Smith during the 1860s. The church is run by the Churches Conservation Trust and is open to visitors. (Author's photograph)

Battlefield Farm and the Battlefield 1403 Visitor Centre are located on the battlefield site. Inside the museum room are several displays and exhibits dedicated to the history of the battle. (Author's photograph)

Several structures have been built on the battlefield since 1403. One of these, Battlefield Farm, is now home to the Battlefield 1403 visitor destination, farm shop and exhibition. Within the exhibition, visitors can find information on the battlefield as well as reproduction armour, weapons and other equipment. From here, a battlefield walk and trail can be followed that guides visitors around the battlefield. Several display panels along the route provide information and historical context. Alternatively, the trail can be started from the Battlefield Heritage Site car park on the A1524.

On the trail visitors will be guided to Battlefield Church, keys for which are kept at the Battlefield 1403 centre. The design of the current church has changed significantly from medieval times but it remains a beautiful and charming sight, without which no visit to the battlefield is complete. In 1406, the rector of Albright Hussey, Roger Yve, was granted a license by Richard Hussey, lord of the same manor, to acquire the land for the

A visitor trail, beginning at the Battlefield 1403 Centre, exists to guide members of the public around the battlefield. Display panels mark the important sites and events of the battle. (Author's photograph)

Henry IV's tomb in Canterbury Cathedral was commissioned by his widow Joan of Navarre around 1425 and remains our best surviving likeness of the king. Joan's effigy was added after her death in 1437. (Author's photograph)

building of a chapel in which masses would be sung for those killed during the battle. By 1409 the original building had been completed. Originally this did not include the tower, which was begun in the 1440s. In 1410, Henry IV established the site as a perpetual chantry complete with a college of priests. The charter established a community of six chaplains and a master to celebrate divine office for the king's soul, as well as those of Richard Hussey, Isolde his wife, and all those killed during the battle. The establishment was also granted the right to present clergy to certain parishes and, for a short time, freedom of taxation; these rights all being confirmed by antipope John XXIII in 1411. The college also included a school and several other buildings, all of which have now disappeared. Evidence of their former presence can be seen in the earthworks and fishponds to the south of the present church, none of which should be mistaken as features present in 1403.

Following the Chantries Act in 1547, the college was demolished and its materials were sold off. The chapel was converted to a parish church during the Reformation and much of its land passed to the Corbet family in 1683. By the 18th century the building was in a bad state of repair but thanks to the generosity of Lady Brinkman, a member of the Corbet family, the church was restored in 1860–62 by the local architect Samuel Pountney Smith. Most of the splendid interior decoration and furnishings date from this time. Among Smith's work is the hammerbeam roof, incorporating the heraldry of knights who fought in the battle, along with the screen, reredos and sedilia. Medieval survivals include the 15th and 16th century stained glass and the 15th century Pietà from Albright Hussey, an image of Our Lady of Pity holding the body of Jesus after his removal from the cross. The exterior of the church has a mixture of decorated and perpendicular architecture, much of which was installed during the repairs. On the east end of the church, above the window, is a 15th-century statue of Henry IV below a canopy and the letters 'H R', standing for 'Henricus Rex'.

BIBLIOGRAPHY

Primary Sources

An English Chronicle 1377–1461, ed. William Marx, Boydell (Woodbridge, 2003)

Calendar of Documents Relating to Scotland, Vol. IV, 1357–1509, ed. Joseph Bain (Edinburgh, 1888)

Calendar of the Close Rolls, Henry IV, Vol. II 1402–5 (London, 1929)

Calendar of the Fine Rolls, Vol. XII. Henry IV, 1399–1405 (London, 1931)

Chronicle of Dieulacres Abbey, ed. M. V. Clarke & V. H. Galbraith. Bulletin of the John Rylands Library (Manchester, 1930)

Chronique du Religieux de Saint-Denys, ed. M. L. Bellaguet (Paris, 1839)

Eulogium Historiarum Sive Temporis, Vol. III, ed. Frank Scott Haydon (London, 1863)

Hall's Chronicle, ed. Henry Ellis (London, 1809)

John Capgraves Abbreuiacion of Cronicles, ed. Peter J. Lucas, Early English Text Society (Oxford, 1983)

J. de Trokelowe et Anon Chronica et Annales. Annales Ricardi Secundi et Henrici Quarti. Rolls Series (1866). Translated in Trans. Shrop. Arch. Soc. Vol. 10. 2nd Series (1898)

John de Waurin's Chronicle, 1399–1422, ed. Sir W. Hardy & Edward L. C. P. Hardy (London, 1887)

Original Letters Illustrative of English History, 2nd Series, Vol. I (London, 1827)

Rymer's Foedera, Vol. II. 1377–1654, ed. Sir Thomas Duffus Hardy (London, 1873)

The Brut or The Chronicles of England, ed. Friedrich W. D. Brie, Part I, Early English Text Society (London, 1906)

The Chronicle of Adam Usk, ed. Chris Given-Wilson, Clarendon Press (Oxford, 1997)

The Chronicle of John Hardyng, ed. R. Grafton & H. Ellis (London, 1812)

The Parliament Rolls of Medieval England 1275–1504, Vol. XIII, Henry IV. 1399–1405, Boydell (London, 2005)

The Chronica Maiora of Thomas Walsingham, Vol. II, 1394–1422, ed. J. Taylor, W. R. Childs & L. Watkiss (Oxford, 2011)

Secondary Sources

Allmand, C., *Henry V*, Yale (1997)

Barratt, J., *War for the Throne: The Battlefield of Shrewsbury 1403*, Pen & Sword (2010)

Bean, J. M. W., *Henry IV and the Percies*, History 44 (1959)

Boardman, A., *Hotspur: Henry Percy Medieval Rebel*, Sutton Press, Stroud (2003)

Boyle, D., *Like Leaves Fall in Autumn: Hotspur, Henry IV & The Battle of Shrewsbury*, Friends of Battlefield Church (2016)

Davies, R. R., The *Revolt of Owain Glyn Dwr*, Oxford University Press (1995)

Dodd, G. & Briggs, D., *Henry IV: The Establishment of the Regime*, Woodbridge (2003)

Fonblanque, E. B., *Annals of the House of Percy*, London (1887)

Fletcher, W. G. D., *Battlefield Church*, Shrewsbury (1903)

Given-Wilson, C., *Henry IV*, Yale (2016)

Griffiths, R., *Prince Henry's War: castles, garrisons and supply during the Glyn rebellion*, B.B.C.S 34 (1987)

Hardy, R. & Strickland, M., *The Great War Bow*, Stroud (2005)

Kirby, J. L., *Henry IV of England*, London (1970)

Lloyd, J. E., *Owen Glendower*, Oxford (1931)

Lomas, R., *The Fall of the House of Percy, 1363–1408*, Edinburgh (2007)

McNiven, P., *The Cheshire Rebellion of 1400*, in *B.J.R.L* 52 (1969–1970)

McNiven, P., *The Men of Cheshire and the Rebellion of 1403*, in *T.L.C.H.S* 129 (1975)

McNiven, P., *The Scottish Policies of the Percies and the Strategy of Rebellion in 1403*, in *B.J.R.L* 62 (1979–1980)

Morgan, P., *War and Society in Medieval Cheshire, 1277–1403*, Manchester (1987)

Mortimer, I., *The Fears of Henry IV*, Vintage (2007)

Pollard, T. & Oliver, N., *Two Men in a Trench: Battlefield Archaeology – The Key to Unlocking the Past*, Penguin (2002)

Prestwich, M., *Armies and Warfare in the Middle Ages: The English Experience*, Yale (1996)

Priestly, E. J., *The Battle of Shrewsbury, 1403*, Shrewsbury (1979)

Wylie, J. H., *History of England under Henry IV*, Vol. I, London (1884)

INDEX